Chrismons Basic Series

Chrismons T.M.

Basic Series

INSTRUCTIONS FOR MAKING THE BASIC SERIES OF CHRISMONS

History, Purpose, Worship Program, Interpretations;
Materials, Patterns, Diagrams, Step-by-Step Directions.

by
Frances Kipps Spencer

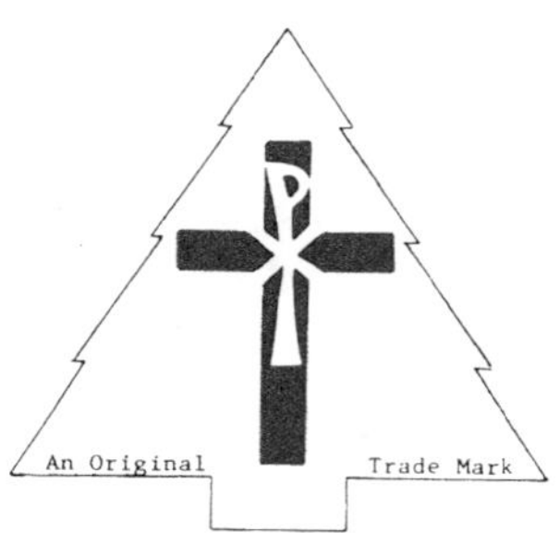

Chrismons speak of our Lord Jesus Christ. Ascension Lutheran Church welcomes you to the growing family of those who make and use these Christian ornaments. May you find the peace of God and joy in His Word as you work with these reminders of His love for all mankind.

Originals of the Chrismons for which patterns and descriptions are given in the following pages hang on the tree in our Church. We of Ascension Church appreciate the opportunity to share the instructions with you. We hope that you will enjoy making Chrismons, that you will find happiness in using them and in giving them to others. Our only limitation is that they not be made for sale.

If you wish to use Chrismons in a church or a non-profit institution, we are glad, on request, to send that organization full permission to use any of our materials (copyright or otherwise) to explain the meaning of the ornaments. Simply send your request with the name and address of the church or institution to us. The copyright release will be forwarded at once.

May God bless you in your desire to keep our Lord at the center of your Christmas celebration.

For the Chrismon Ministry Team
at Ascension Lutheran Church
Danville, Virginia, U.S.A.

CREDITS

PHOTOGRAPHS:
Richard H. Craigue

PUBLICATION:
Kit W. Barkhouser
Gail K. Bengston
Gary L. Bengston
Roy B. Burnett, Jr.
Anna D. Evans
Mary Lee E. Gravely
Robert F. Holley
Judy E. Johnson
Undine H. Kipps
Encie A. Napier
Robert V. Shaver
Harry W. Spencer
Jean K. Stahl
Kim M. Stahl

CHRISMONS: BASIC SERIES

Fourth Edition, Revised
First Printing

Published by The Ascension Lutheran Church
314 West Main Street, Danville, Virgina 24541, U.S.A.

Printed in the United States of America
by Piedmont Printing & Graphics, Danville, Virginia

ISBN 0-9715472-0-3
www.chrismon.org chrismon@gamewood.net

CONTENTS

THE CHRISMON CHRISTMAS TREE: History, Definition, Purpose

When did the Chrismon tree begin? And why? What is the reason for it? Where did the idea originate?

It began as an offering to God. God blessed the offering, and it became a song of praise and thanksgiving to Him. It continues as a witness to His love and His glory, as a proclamation of His holy Name through His Son, Jesus, the Christ, our Lord.

When we look back, we see one beginning of the tree during the Christmas season of 1940. An elderly minister, the Reverend George Pass, came by our home to wish us a Merry Christmas. He saw the discarded Christmas gift wrappings and asked for them. He wanted to use the pretty papers and ribbons to make Christmas ornaments for a tree in his little church. There was no money to buy decorations; but there was a willingness to glorify God with the talents which he had and the materials that he could get.

Mr. Pass's devotion moved us. For some years after that, it was difficult to buy ornaments to decorate our home tree. But we still wanted a Christmas tree. So, my husband and I began to make our tree decorations. Each year there was a different tree; every Christmas we became more proficient in using various materials to carry out our ideas. Because of the minister's inspiration, I became a semi-professional at creating new and unusual Christmas trees.

The earliest beginning was, of course, in my home as a child. The tree in the house always seemed more beautiful than anyone else's. My parents, I knew, worked hard to make it so. As far back as I can remember, there was also the Christmas at church. I recall no trees in the church during my early childhood. The tree stood for a different kind of celebration than the one in which people participated at church. Later, when I saw Christmas trees in churches, I ignored them as being out of place.

In 1956 there was a tree in the Lutheran Church of the Ascension that I did not ignore. It was not unusual; it was the kind of tree with colored lights and balls that one saw anywhere at Christmas time. But that year I saw, and appreciated, the people behind the tree. That tree made me aware of those members who cared enough to do what they could; I again recognized the simple and profound dedication of being willing to give. And the one who was a professional was giving nothing. Because I was not willing to participate, the congregation was not making its full offering.

The next beginning was the following spring when I volunteered to decorate the tree in the Church, and the pastor accepted the offer. I had no ideas or plans except to try, with the ability which God had given me, to create something more suitable for the Church. Months went by while I tried to think of a way to do the job; many ideas came and were discarded; none were good enough.

Then, perhaps, came the real beginning; I realized that Christmas was the birthday of the Christ Child. Suppose it had been the custom in His day and time to decorate birthday cakes for children? How would Mary have decorated a cake for Son Jesus? His name, yes. But what else would please Him?

That was the answer; Let the Child be honored, the Person He is! Oh, there were weeks of research before the Chrismons came to my attention. I knew nothing of Christian symbolism. But now I knew what I was doing, what I wanted to say. Since then, the glory of God and His love have been and are the song which we sing through the Chrismon tree. We talk about the Gift that He gave us that day. We say what we can where we are, with the materials which He gives us; we say it to the people around us, in their language; and we try to help others sing a similar song. This is the Chrismon idea.

* * *

While searching for a way to honor the Christ, I came across some drawings of designs called chrisma. "Chrismon" is a combination of parts of two words: CHRISt and MONogram. A Chrismon is just that—a monogram of Christ.

(According to the dictionary definition, a chrismon (krĭz′ mŏn) is the Chi Rho monogram of Christ. The plural is chrisma; the word is not capitalized. Ascension Lutheran Church adopted this word to designate the special Christmas tree ornaments that this Church developed because the first designs were all based on chrisma. In this usage, the word Chrismon is capitalized, and the plural is Anglicized to Chrismons. Over the years these ornaments have developed so that now a Chrismon may be a monogram, a sign, a symbol, a type, or a combination of such figures. The one requirement is that it refer primarily to our Lord and God.)

The black and white prints that I found were copies of chrisma designed and carved or drawn by some of the earliest Christians. These monograms were discovered in many places—some on jewelry or utensils, others on doors or buildings, and still more on the walls of the catacombs in Rome. Early Christians used them to identify themselves to one another, to designate meeting places of the church, and, sometimes, to show unbelievers where they stood. Even more important, these symbols of the early church served to transmit the faith and beliefs of the artist-teacher to the viewer. Thus the inspiration was shared and passed on.

From an artistic viewpoint, the designs were quite beautiful. It was apparent that they would make lovely Christmas tree decorations. More than that, though, it occurred to us that, by using these early signs of our faith to decorate the tree, we would bring out distinctly the real reason that we celebrate this day of the year. Further, we hoped that such a Christmas tree would not only be worthy of being placed in the Lord's house but would also contribute to the spirit of worship in this holy season.

While the original idea had been to use only monograms of Christ to decorate the tree, a few other symbols of the early church were added to tell a more complete story. Because Christmas (Christ + mass) is a celebration of His festival, designs were limited to those which referred primarily to Him. Because we wanted the tree to speak directly to anyone who happened to come into the Church, designs which pointed to denominations were omitted. The first Chrismon tree in the nave of our Church in 1957 held only a dozen different ornaments. We thought that the story of the Christ was told symbolically.

But we found that the more we grew as Christians, the more we had to say about our Lord. In 1958, some new Chrismons were added to the tree. When the same thing happened in 1959, we realized that our tree would never be completed. There is always something new to say about God, always a better way to say it. Through the ages the church has found varied ways of telling the Good News, and the living church of today will find still other ways of making God's love more meaningful and apparent to humanity.

We affirm these beliefs in our decoration of the Chrismon tree at Ascension Church by adding new designs each year. Some of the new ornaments are developed from symbols of the church in its earliest years. Others were first used by the inspired writers of the Bible. And still others are new interpretations which add depth to our understanding of our Lord and our relationship to Him. But we have always insisted that any symbol on the tree must, first of all, point to our Lord and God.

All Chrismons are made in combinations of white and gold. White, the liturgical color for Christmas, refers to our Lord's purity and perfection; gold, to His majesty and glory. We point to the Christ as the Light of the world by using tiny white lights on the tree.

* * *

The patterns in this book cover Chrismons designed for and used on the tree at The Lutheran Church of the Ascension in Danville, Virginia, from 1957 through 1964. Chrismons carefully made by these directions and suggestions have a professional appearance. From the comments of those who have seen them, the designs and their materials have ample variety to satisfy the average church-goer. At the same time, the tree has the dignity and beauty to make it appropriate for use in a house of worship.

These decorations can easily be simplified, made more elaborately, or redesigned completely without violating the basic principle of the tree. The place in which the tree is shown and the personal taste of those for whom it is decorated should be factors in deciding what changes to make. If the tree is planned for a church, keep in mind the fact that the church is God's house; make the tree worthy of being placed there. Wherever the Chrismons are placed, remember that they speak of our Lord and God; they are a song of and to the Glory of God.

If this is the first year for a Chrismon tree, it may be better to concentrate on the easier ornaments in the beginning and add more difficult ones in following years. (See page 12.) To attempt to make all the designs in one year would be too difficult for most groups. In addition, most people are not sufficiently educated concerning Christian symbolism to take in all the meanings at once. The practice of adding new Chrismons each year gives time to develop skill in making them and enables a group to gradually acquire an understanding of what the tree says. Most of all, this method keeps the tree and its message fresh and new and alive to one's fellow worshipers. For is not a live, vital witness necessary to the development of a live and vital Christian?

No particular artistic skill is needed to make Chrismons, although one should have the self-discipline to work carefully. Any woman or girl who can sew well enough to make a dress for herself, any man or boy who can fashion a window screen, or any person who can play a hymn on a piano has all the manual dexterity that is needed. The first few designs may go slowly, but speed will soon be gained. Of course, it will take time, but it is a pleasant task. My only hope is that Chrismon makers find half as much joy in making these decorations as I did.

We hope that the time comes when you create some of your own designs for your tree. Many books (pastors can recommend some) on Christian symbolism are full of ideas. As one works thoughtfully with the materials, inspirations come faster than they can be developed. Try to work out the best of them. During the creative process, remember the basic principles, meaning, and intent of the tree. New Chrismons that are made in this way may become not only the most meaningful and cherished ones on a tree but may also serve as inspirations for others to follow.

* * *

The Chrismon tree is complete only when those who see it understand its meaning. If the tree is in a public place, an explanation of its symbolism such as is shown on pages 3 and 4 should be given to those who see the tree. In fact, one of the most surprising aspects of the program is the care with which people study the explanation and the tree so that they can interpret each symbol. Because only those symbols that appear on the tree are interpreted, explanations may, for a year or two, be shorter than the following. As the tree grows in later years, the interpretation will be longer.

DO NOT FORGET THIS EXPLANATION! IT IS VITAL!

THE SYMBOLISM OF OUR CHRISTMAS TREE

Welcome to the Lutheran Church of the Ascension.
May you each be blessed with the love and joy and true meaning of Christmas.

This year, again, our tree is decorated with the symbols from Christian history which refer to our Lord and Savior, Jesus Christ. They tell the story of God's plan for our salvation that, through faith in Jesus Christ, we might all be restored to the Father in a community of love, the Christian Church.

SYMBOLISM OF THE CHRISTIAN YEAR SERIES

The symbols grouped on the large double loop are based on the Church Year, which follows the Life of our Lord. The upper circle tells about God while the lower loop, read counterclockwise, depicts the Life through Which God was revealed to all mankind for all time.

ADVENT — "The Scroll with Prophecy." Isaiah 9:6.

CHRISTMAS — "Gladiolus." The Incarnation, the Word became flesh. John 1:1, 1:14. The living Word, the living Sword. Hebrews 4:12.

EPIPHANY — "Five-point Star." The manifestation to the Wise Men. Matthew 2:2. A star out of Jacob. Numbers 24:17. Also see Revelation 22:16.

LENT — "Pelican-in-her-piety." The Atonement (Sacrifice of Christ for our sins); the Lord's Supper. Psalm 102:6 (K.J.) or 101:7 (Douay); Matthew 26:27, 28.

EASTER — "Phoenix Rising from Flames." The Resurrection. I Corinthians 15:3, 4. From Egyptian fables concerning a miraculous bird which would destroy itself in flames only to rise again to a new life in three days; a symbol of immortality.

ASCENSION — "Chariot of Fire." The ascension of Elijah (II Kings 2:11) parallels the ascension of our Lord in Acts 1:9-11.

PENTECOST — "Seven-tongued Flame." The Holy Spirit on the Day of Pentecost. Acts 2:1-4. Seven gifts of the Spirit. Isaiah 11:2; Revelation 5:12.

TRINITY — "Triangle with Shamrock and Shells." The Triune God. Matthew 28:19.

GOD, THE FATHER — "The Hand." Psalm 98:1 (Douay 97:1); 139:10 (D. 138:10); I Peter 5:6.

GOD, THE SON — "The Lamb of God." Isaiah 53:7; John 1:29; Revelation 5:12.

GOD, THE SPIRIT — "The Descending Dove." John 1:32-34.

CHALICE ON SIX-POINT STAR — The Lord's Supper. Mark 14:22; Isaiah 11:2.

SHELL ON EIGHT-POINT STAR — Holy Baptism. Matthew 28:19; I Peter 3:20, 21.

BOOK ON SEVEN-POINT STAR — The written Word, the inspired Scripture.

The VINE which connects the symbols of the LIFE is from John 15:1-5. For the nine FRUITS of the Spirit, see Galations 5:22.

THE CROSS

is, of course, always a reminder of our Lord's saving work of redeeming mankind through His sacrifice for our sins, thereby bringing forgiveness and salvation. Different forms of the cross may point to various aspects of our Christ's life and work.

CROSSES on the Christian Year Figure

— TAU CROSS (Anticipatory, Old Testament, Advent). Salvation promised but not yet accomplished. Numbers 21:9; Isaiah 53.

— ANCHOR CROSS (Cross of Hope). This Child, the hope of the world; or, a cross rises from a crescent moon, a symbol for our Lord's mother. Hebrews 6:19; Luke 2:7.

— CROSS CROSSLET. The spread of Christianity to the North, East, South, and West—to the ends of the earth. Matthew 28:19; Mark 8:34; Acts 1:8.

— PASSION CROSS (Cross of Suffering). Pointed ends remind of the points of the nails, the thorns, and the spear. John 19.

— CROSS IN GLORY (Rayed, Easter). The rising sun behind the cross suggests the new day when our Lord conquered death by His Resurrection. I Corinthians 15. 2.

— CROSS OF CONSTANTINE. The Chi Rho with the X turned to form a cross; Christ the conquering King. I Timothy 6:15.

— CROSS FLAMANT (Fiery Cross). Flames signify the fiery zeal of one filled with the Spirit of God. Romans 12:11.

— CROSS TREFLÉE (Bottonnée). Three circles at the end of each arm symbolize the Holy Trinity. II Corinthians 13:14.

— ST. ANDREW'S CROSS. Andrew was reputed to have died on a cross of this shape. Here, this cross symbolizes the whole Christian Church. Ephesians 1:23.

OTHER CROSSES ON THE CHRISMON TREE

— LATIN CROSS, long upright; most widely used form of the cross among Christians.

— GREEK CROSS, all extensions of equal length. This balanced form is easier to use in designs and was much employed by early Greek artists.

— CROSS OVER THE WORLD. Christ over the world, "Go ye into all the world . . ."

— JERUSALEM CROSS. Four Tau crosses meet to form a larger cross: Five wounds of our Lord. Or, Old Testament prophecies (Tau's) culminated in the crucifixion of our Lord (large cross) on a hill near Jerusalem. Since then His followers have carried the Gospel to the corners of the world (small corner crosses).

— CROSS TRIUMPHANT. A world united in Christ; triumph of the Lord over earthly sin.

— CROSS PATÉE with Four Scrolls. Our salvation as proclaimed in the four Gospels. Winged man, Matthew; winged lion, Mark; winged ox, Luke; eagle, John.

— CROSS IN ETERNITY.

MONOGRAMS, LETTERS, and WORDS

The earliest monograms of our Lord are in Greek letters. Originally much of the New Testament was written in Greek because many of the first missionary churches were Greek.

X — Chi, the first letter of the word for CHrist in Greek.

XP — Chi Rho, the first letters of CHRist in the Greek alphabet. Or, for the Latin *Christus Rex*, Christ the King. The X may sometimes become a cross.

IHC, IHS — First three letters of JESus in Greek. (Note: Some letters have several forms.)

✱, IX — Mongram of the first letters of Jesus and CHrist; our Lord's cipher.

A Ω — Alpha and Omega, the first and last letters of the Greek alphabet. Since only God is be-
or a w fore and after all things, a symbol of divinity. Revelation 22:13.

INRI — The first letters of the words in the Latin superscription, "Jesus of Nazareth, King of the Jews." John 19:19.

NIKA — The Greek word for conquer or conqueror or victor.

M — The first letter of the name of our Lord's mother, Mary.

SYMBOLS FOR OUR LORD AND GOD

△ — An equilateral triangle, three-part figure, or any three like items — The Triune God.

○ — A circle symbolizes eternity; God, the only eternal One, or eternal life with God.

CROWN — The Kingship of our Lord Christ Jesus; His victory over sin and death; His place of honor at the right hand of God. I Timothy 6:15; Revelation 14:14; Romans 8:34.

CORNERSTONE — "Jesus Christ, the chief corner stone." Ephesians 2:20.

SUN OF RIGHTEOUSNESS — Our Lord as prophecied in Malachi 4:2.

STARS — When formed by crosses set at angles, stars suggest the close relationship between the birth and death of our Lord. FIVE-point, Epiphany; SIX-point, Creator's; SEVEN-point, Gifts of the Spirit; EIGHT-point, Regeneration through Holy Baptism.

FISH — *IXΘYC (ICHTHUS)*, the Greek word for fish forms an acrostic on the first letters of, "Jesus Christ, God's Son, Savior." One of the most ancient symbols for our Lord.

SERPENT on a TAU CROSS — Prefiguration of the sacrifice on the cross. John 3:14.

BUTTERFLY — Our Lord's Resurrection; also the resurrection of those who die in Christ.

WHEAT & GRAPES — Bread and wine; the Body and Blood of our Lord. Luke 22:17-20.

THORNS — A representation of our Lord's crown of suffering. Mark 15:17.

ROSE — The Nativity of our Lord. Also our Lord's mother, Mary. Isaiah 35:1. (K.J.)

DAISY — The innocence of the Christ-Child.

LILY-OF-THE-VALLEY — The humility of the man Jesus. Song of Solomon 2:1.

There are various combinations of these monograms, symbols, and crosses on our tree, but these are the basic elements. All of the Chrismons used to decorate the tree are in white and gold to symbolize the purity and perfection, the majesty and glory of the Son of God.

MAY THESE SYMBOLS CONTINUALLY REMIND YOU OF GOD'S GREATEST GIFT TO US ALL, JESUS CHRIST.

If you would like further information concerning the faith here expressed during this Holy Season, please call on the Pastor at any time. You are invited to worship with us on Christmas Eve at the Candlelight Service at 11:00 P.M.

THE NATIVITY OF OUR LORD, CHRISTMAS

The Lutheran Church of the Ascension

314 West Main Street, Danville, Virginia 24541, U.S.A.

THE CHILD WE HONOR: A Christmas Program

In response to requests for programs to explain the meaning of the Chrismons, this simple pageant is included. It can be presented with only two speakers—one to read the leader's parts and the other to make the responses. Or, one person can give the leader's lines while different individuals read the various responses. To make the program more elaborate, a living pantomime of the manger scene could be added.

* * *

It is suggested that the Chrismons be shown to the audience by the person who gives the response. When the notation *(Hang)* appears, the Chrismon is handed to another individual who hangs it on the tree. (The same "hanger" places all the Chrismons in the program on the tree.) If the tree is completely decorated before the program, let a "spotter" who is in one of the front pews shine a spotlight (sealed beam flashlight) on the Chrismon that is being described.

The exact Chrismon that is named in italics with the *Hang* direction need not be used. For example, it is only necessary that the first Chrismon have a rose on it, that the second have an IHC or IHS, that the third have the XP, and so on. The capitalized word in the lead line of the response lists the idea that must appear or be symbolized in the Chrismon that is shown.

* * *

Words of the carols are an integral part of this program. The audience can sing all of them, or their presentation may be varied as noted in the program.

Not all versions of "What Child Is This?" have a stanza that contains a reference to the crucifixion. Because this stanza is necessary to the sense of the program, it is printed below by permission of Simon and Schuster from *Fireside Book of Folk Songs,* copyright 1947; words by H. C. Dix.

"Why lies He in such mean estate,
Where ox and ass are feeding?
Good Christian, fear, for sinners here
The silent word is pleading;
Nails, spear, shall pierce Him through,
The Cross be borne for me, for you:
Hail, hail, the Word made flesh,
The Babe, the Son of Mary."

* * *

The program was originally presented to an interdenominational group of women ranging in age from the teens to the eighties. If it is given to a group of other composition, some lines at the end of the leader's last talk must be changed. Ways to worship and adore the Child should be activities in which the average member of the audience normally engages.

Try to give each person in the audience a copy of the following program. If desired, the names of the participants and the words of the carols sung by the audience may be included.

Program for:

THE CHILD WE HONOR

Prelude: Christmas Carols .... Chorus

THE ROSE IN THE DESERT .... Leader

"Lo, How a Rose E'er Blooming" .... Solo

WHO IS THIS CHILD?

Jesus
The Christ
The Morning Star
The Son of God
The Sun of Righteousness
The King of kings

"Hark, the Herald Angels Sing" .... Audience

WHAT IS THIS CHILD TO DO?

To die on the Cross
To lie in a Tomb
To conquer Sin and Death

"What Child Is This?" .... Chorus

WHAT DOES THIS CHILD GIVE?

New Life
Divine Love
Perfect Joy

"O, Come All Ye Faithful" .... Audience

THE CHILD WE HONOR

Christmas Carols: Chorus.

Leader:

In the beginning, God was. He created heaven and earth, and earth was a paradise. Afterwards, He created man in His own image and set him in this paradise. God and man walked together.

Then man decided that he preferred his own way to God's will, and man disobeyed God. By this sin, man separated himself from his Creator. The earth became a wilderness, and man was lost in the barren desert of his own sin.

Although man had turned his back on his Maker, God still loved him. The Father looked on His people and had compassion on them. Out of His love, God made a plan for man's salvation and revealed it through His prophets. This was the prophecy of Isaiah, a spokesman for the Lord:

"The wilderness, and the solitary place, shall be glad for them: And the desert shall rejoice, and blossom as the rose. It shall blossom abundantly, and rejoice even with joy and singing." *(Hang: CROSS & CHI OF ROSES.)*

Vocal Solo: "Lo, How a Rose E'er Blooming."

Leader:

Isaiah's prophecy that the desert would blossom as the rose was fulfilled when a Child was born in Bethlehem of Judea. Who did they say that this Child was?

Response for JESUS:

"She brought forth her first-born, and wrapped Him in swaddling clothes, and laid Him in a manger . . . And, when eight days were accomplished for the circumcising of the Child, His name was called Jesus, which was so named of the angel before He was conceived in the womb."

(Hang IHS in Circle.)

A century later, His followers made monograms of the first three letters of His name in Greek, the language of the world of that time. To this day, those who follow the Infant Who lay in the manger still use this monogram of His given name.

Response for the CHRIST:

The night that He was born was glorious to shepherds on the hills outside Bethlehem. An angel appeared to them and said, "Unto you is born a Savior Who is Christ the Lord."

(Hang XP with Alpha & Omega.)

Christ is the title for the Messiah Whom God promised to send to redeem His people. The Greek monogram of the first letters of Christ, Chi Rho, was the most widely used early Christian symbol. Those who recognize the Babe as their Lord and personal Redeemer still use the Greek Chi, which looks like the Latin X, to identify themselves as His followers.

Response for The STAR:

This is the sacred cipher which combines the first letter of our Lord's given name, Jesus, with the first letter of His title, Christ. This design is often called a star. The star, in turn, reminds us of how our Savior described Himself. One of the Messianic prophecies, "There shall come a star out of Jacob," *(Hang the Iota Chi, the I on top of the X).* was answered by our Lord Himself in the Revelation of St. John the Divine with the words, "I am the bright and morning star."

Leader:

A Child was born—the Messiah promised by God came to deliver mankind. Was that the reason the angels sang that night? Was that the Glory of Christmas?

Response for The SON OF GOD:

The answer is here—in the circle that surrounds the sacred cipher. Since a circle has no beginning and no end, it may symbolize eternity

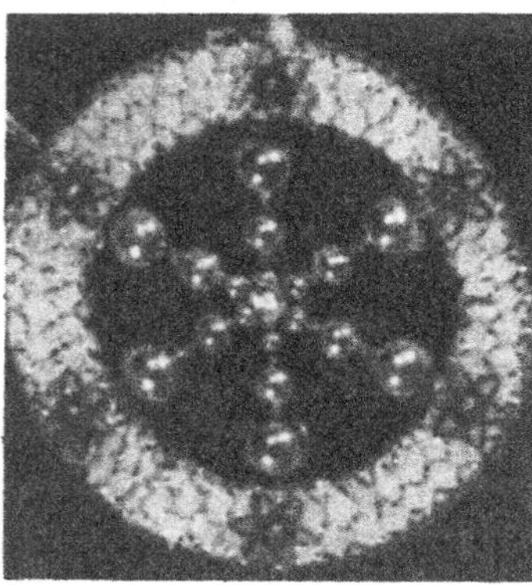

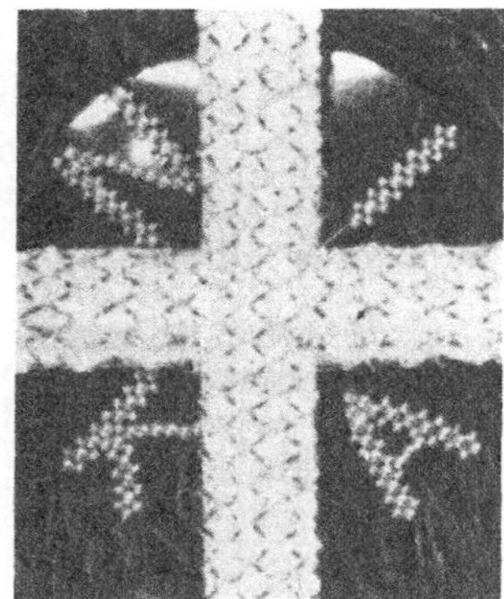

and, by extension, God, the only eternal one.
(Hang Iota Chi in a Circle.)

Response for The SUN OF RIGHTEOUSNESS:

He is the Sun of Righteousness promised in the book of Malachi. "For unto you who fear my name, the Sun of Righteousness shall rise with healing in His wings."
(Hang the Sun of Righteousness.)

Response for the KING OF KINGS:

He is the King of Kings and the Lord of lords. With the angels we sing to the glory of the new-born King, for the Babe is God, the Lord, the Ruler of the whole earth and all the heavens.

Group Hymn: "Hark the Herald Angels Sing."

Leader:

So much promised for a Child! It is right that we honor Him, for the glory of God is about Him. But the love of God is greater than His glory and power. For, in that love, He laid aside His power and glory.

Response for TO DIE:

In humility, He laid aside His power. In love, He took up the cross for you and for me.
(Hang the Greek Cross.)
By His death on the cross, He atoned for our sins.

Leader:

The Infant Who was named Jesus was to die on the cross. This rose of love that bloomed in the desert of sin was to fade and die to bring healing life and light to the wilderness. The promised Messiah was born to die on the cross.

Response for TO LIE IN A TOMB:

The Man Who hung on the cross was the eternal One—the Alpha and the Omega—the beginning and the end. The Son of God hung on the cross; God gave us His only Son to die for us—and they laid Him in the tomb.
(Hang the Latin Cross with Alpha and Omega.)

Response for TO CONQUER SIN AND DEATH:

But the sinless One conquered sin and death. Just as the lowly larva lies encased in the seemingly dead chrysalis only to emerge as a glorious butterfly, our Lord lay in the tomb only to vanquish sin and death for us. On the third day He burst forth triumphantly from the tomb.
(Hang the Butterfly on Cross and Chi in Circle.)

He won the victory for us, so that we who believe may share eternal life with Him. This was the work of the Child Who lay sleeping on the Virgin's lap.

Vocal Chorus: "What Child Is This?"

Response for NEW LIFE:

Because of the life and death of this Baby, the Son of Mary and the Son of God, we, who were creatures of God, may become children of God. The eight-pointed star symbolizes our regeneration through Holy Baptism. We who were dead have a new life in the Christ.
(Hang the Eight-pointed Star.)

Response for DIVINE LOVE:

So we of the world enthrone the King of salvation in our hearts. He, Who could have conquered all in power, chose instead to give Himself in love. This is the joy of Christmas which is to all men, for divine love came down from heaven to live on earth.
(Hang the Cross atop the World.)

Leader:

This is our perfect joy not only during the Christmas season but throughout the whole year. At this time, though, the joy seems most vivid, for when we contemplate the Holy Infant, God's love is most near. We Christians reflect this gladness in our lives; we do happy things: We sing special songs; we give gifts to those whom we love and to those whom we do not even know; we smile and laugh more often; we even decorate our surroundings to reflect the joy in our hearts. For the gladness cannot be restained.

The love of God is too big to be held in one heart. We who know that love must give it to others. Sometimes we may think only of the joy and forget why we rejoice. Then we must go back to the manger to recall again Who the Infant is and what He is to do. We must commit ourselves into His hands again.

Today, for a little while, we are together to think about God's plan. We look to the holy Child in the manger. We honor Him Who needs no honor. We worship Him with hands and words and songs and hearts. But this is only a small part of our worship in this season of the holy day; this is merely the beginning. Only when we honor Him with our whole lives is our gift worthy.

Let us dare to let our whole being reflect the joy of worshiping the Christ. Let us worship as we talk with our neighbors, as we smile to members of our families or to strangers. Let us adore Him when we wash dishes or type letters or give or sell a service to another. Let us honor Him when we love one another and when we express that love with lips or hands or heart.

God's plan began in love with the birth of a Child in a stable. Through His grace, we have the privilege of being a part of it. Let us begin by honoring the Child. Oh, come, let us worship the Lord! Let us adore Him!

Group Hymn: "O, Come All Ye Faithful."

THE CHILDREN'S CORNER

(Photograph: Page 69.)

Some groups (Ascension Church was one) used to be dubious about a Chrismon tree's appeal to children. Experience shows, however, that fears about a child's ability to appreciate the tree are unjustified. A group in Pennsylvania reported these words of a thirteen year old boy. "Why hasn't this been done before? It's prettier than a regular tree and makes more sense."

By the age of ten, the average child can understand the meaning of the symbols. What the youngster may lack in knowledge and experience is compensated for by a freer imagination and flexibility. Even a younger child can be stirred by the unusual beauty of the Chrismons. A mother overheard her daughter's five year old playmate say, "I wish my mother was a Lutheran. Then I could help her make Chrismons."

For the most part though, while younger children know that a Chrismon tree is something "special," something to do with God, they do not understand its deeper significance. To reach this group, Ascension has decorated a section of the tree as the "Children's Corner." The essentials of this communication with youngsters have been: A special central Chrismon (a creche or manger scene), miniature size and simplicity of the surrounding ornaments, proper placement of the Corner, and its presentation to the children.

* * *

At the center of the Chrismons that comprise the children's section is a creche. A shed of pieces of bark or painted cardboard is glued to a six by four inch green styrofoam oval. The foam is flat on top and curved to a depth of an inch and a half at its deepest. Pieces of straw are pasted to the foam to make the stable floor. The Child in the manger and Mary and Joseph are placed in the shelter; a few lambs stand near by; bushes and trees are pieces of artificial greenery. The scene is small (Joseph is only an inch and a half high) and simple without extra figures to clutter it. The styrofoam with the arrangement on it is suspended in an eight inch diameter wire circle wrapped with gold vinyl festooning. (See the Chi and Cross in two Circles.) Children who have any religious training at all immediately recognize the Baby Jesus.

The creche is hung on the tree at a five year old child's eye level. Around the scene are small Chrismons from one to four inches high. Their size impresses children with the fact that this area is especially for them. Keep these Chrismons simple in design and execution to avoid visual distractions and involved meanings: A cross of a few beads, a glittered styrofoam fish, a simple star, and so on. The miniature Chrismons for which directions are given in *Chrismons for Every Day* are ideal to use here. The whole decorated children's area occupies a space of about three square feet.

Place the Children's Corner low on the tree where a child can get close to it and see it easily without craning. It is a treat to see the amusement in a youngster's eyes when the child becomes aware that, to see the Baby Jesus, it is the grown-up who must get "out-of-joint." And it does not hurt an adult to discover that he must kneel to look at the Holy Infant.

Recently Ascension Church added a music box to the Children's Corner. The three inch plain gold ball plays "Silent Night, Holy Night" when it climbs its cord after a ring attached to the cord atop the ball has been pulled out. The ball could become a Cross Triumphant to hang on the tree. Such usage, however, would necessitate an adult's care in pulling the ball to make it play. So that children could play the box, it was left plain, and the ring was tied to a three inch metal angle fastened, about nine inches above the floor, on a wall next to the Children's Corner. Children are invited to push the ball to the floor to play a lullaby for Baby Jesus. They cannot pull the string too far out, jerk the tree, or damage any decorated surface. This ball can be seen at the lower left on the front cover picture of *Chrismons.*

Finally, give the children what has been created for them. At St. Andrew's in Charleston, South Carolina, a child may even pick up the baby and hold it. One may not wish to go that far. But when a child comes into the church, take him to the tree and tell him that this part was made especially for him. If adults are in the way, ask them to step aside to let an important person see. If more or less formal explanations are the custom, after the talk is finished and before the questions begin, look over the group for youngsters. Ask them to go to the tree with you to see what is there for them. Then, so that you do not neglect your own education, as the children look where you point, watch their faces.

A note to you--

Wouldn't it be wonderful if we could meet face to face? You could ask all the questions that are running through your mind; I could get to know you personally. Such a meeting, however, is unlikely and, from your point of view, unnecessary.

You see, I already know what many of your questions would be. I have had the pleasure of talking to many of you--and answering your questions--over the years. Replies to nineteen out of twenty of those queries are on the next few pages of this book! So--what new thing would I say if we two could meet and talk?

First, I would say, take it easy! Everything need not be learned at once. The best beginning is to skim over the General Information on pages 9 to 16. You need not read all the words, but note what information is available--and where.

Second, look over the Construction Techniques on page 16 through 20 BEFORE you make any Chrismons. Instead of repeating frequently used procedures in the directions, they are described once in this section. Find out what procedures are explained here and learn when you should refer to them.

Third, you CAN DO it! Thousands of people around the world have made Chrismons with no help beyond this book. Merely reading the directions for a Chrismon confuses you? They are not written to amuse; they are given to be followed! Chrismon makers have written: "If one just sits down with the materials and follows the instructions step-by-step, it is easy."

Finally, enjoy yourself, your work! Making Chrismons can be an act of worship of our Lord and God. Let it be so for you. Whatever form your worship of the Christ takes, be happy in it.

Yours in Christ,

Frances Spencer

THE EVERGREEN TREE

Kinds of Tree or Trees:

It is generally best to have the same kind of evergreen that is usual in a specific locality. When this is done, one shows symbolically that the Good News of the Christ is valid for any culture in which one happens to be. On the practical side, it is likely that the most suitable species available in an area is already being used. Any evergreen can symbolize eternal life.

When a locality can choose from several varieties, the tree with the thickest, most compact greenery should be selected for Chrismon use. Thin, straggly trees allow glimpses of the backs of decorations on opposite sides of the tree to show through. If other decorations show through, they detract from the clarity of the message of another ornament. Chrismon trees must provide the best possible background for each design.

Some congregations prefer the formal balance of two trees, one on each side of the chancel. The only time such a practice causes concern to Chrismon tree decorators is when they use the Christian Year Series. The instructions in that book gives specific directions on how to adapt the Christian Year Chrismons to two trees.

The Tree After Christmas:

Churches and homes use Chrismons as teaching tools and Christian decorations throughout the year. The tree on which the Chrismons hang can also bring a message at another season. Converting a Christmas tree to a rough cross which, during Lent, stands where the tree stood at Christmas is not original with Ascension Church. Nevertheless this potent way to show what people may do with God's gifts should be passed on.

After the Christmas Tree is taken down, cut the branches off the trunk. Saw the trunk into two pieces to make the upright and arm beam. Nail the pieces together to make a properly proportioned cross. Do not try to smooth out the trunk to cover the scars; it will not be the first time that wounds showed. Either stand or hang the cross where the tree stood.

On Easter Day, this same cross can symbolize how God is willing to cover even the worst sins with the righteousness of His Son. With white lilies and green ivy, decorate the bare, barren ugly cross to convert it to the Easter Cross, the Cross in Glory. The wood is not covered entirely; it is made to look as if it had come to life, as if flowers were growing out of it. When the worshiper walks into the church on Easter morning and becomes aware of the beauty in that shadowed corner where the ugliness of Lent stood before, he or she experiences a joy that exceeds even the gladness of Christmas.

* * *

Any spring blooming bulb can be used on the cross as well as the lilies. Likewise, any greenery will serve as well as ivy. To keep the ivy fresh throughout Easter Day, soak it in a tub of water for a day before stapling it to the cross on Easter Eve day. Blossoms will stay fresh if they are put in water in rubber stoppered florist's tubes. Before the flower is put in a tube, wrap the end of a 12 or 18 inch piece of stranded wire to hold around the tube. Then cover the tube and its leftover wire with stretchable green florist tape. After the tube is filled with water and stoppered, insert the flower. Attach the tubed flower to the cross by stapling the leftover wire in place.

Instead of flowers, Chrismons suitable for the Easter Season may be placed on the cross.

SIZES OF CHRISMONS

The patterns in this book are the size of the decorations that are placed on a church tree. While some of them may seem large, it is necessary that, for a tree in an auditorium, the designs be easily recognized from a distance. Smaller ornaments, Chrismons B, C, D, and Y, for example, are scattered as fillers among medium size and large symbols. Home size designs may also be made for use as small fillers.

If the tree is less than 12 feet tall, reduce the size of the larger Chrismons unless the design of an ornament does not lend itself to such a reduction. When making Chrismons for a tree in a room of average size, use the half or home size patterns. Miniature Chrismons are suitable for use as fillers on such a tree. Miniatures may also be used on small table trees or in a "Children's Corner" on either a room size or a large church tree. (Patterns for some miniatures are on the supplementary sheet, 'Chrismon Miniatures," Form G. More complete directions and patterns for miniatures are in *Chrismons for Every Day.*)

NUMBER OF CHRISMONS NEEDED

One of the most frequently asked questions is, "How many Chrismons are needed to decorate a tree?" Before a reply can be made, however, other questions must be answered. "What size tree? What kind of tree? Where is it to stand?" Answers to these and other questions must be known and correlated before any estimate can be made. These variables are discussed below.

* * *

Density of Decorations:

Many people feel that hanging more ornaments on a tree makes it more beautiful. Ascension Church found that too many Chrismons led to confusion; over-decorated trees are difficult to interpret. Too many lights actually prevent one from seeing and identifying the designs. Furthermore, the artistry of a more lightly decorated tree on which each symbol has its own surrounding greenery is preferred in Danville.

If one would err in this matter, it is better to underdecorate than the reverse. As ornaments become more beautiful and detailed, viewers seem to want fewer of them on the tree. Acquisition of quality lessens the desire for quantity. Sparsely decorated trees, of course, require fewer Chrismons than heavily ornamented ones.

Placement of the Tree:

A tree set in a corner so that two of its sides are hidden requires only about three-fifths the decorations that a tree in the middle of a room needs. If the tree is against a wall, it requires about four-fifths of the Chrismons that would be needed for a tree decorated around its full circumference.

Species of the Tree:

Some evergreens are, by their nature, denser and more evenly shaped than others. These trees require more Chrismons than those with branches that jut out into the air. Irregular and thin trees need fewer ornaments because, since they are more open, Chrismons on the opposite sides of branches are more easily glimpsed. When too many ornaments hang on an open tree, their designs cannot be distinguished from one another. Dense, even trees that have fewer "holes" have more greenery background for more Chrismons.

Height of the Tree:

Taller trees obviously require more ornaments than shorter trees. Remember, however, that the extra height of a tree that is thin at the top requires fewer ornaments than one that is thick all the way up. Likewise, trees that bush out widely at the base can support more decorations than those that are slim to the bottom.

* * *

The preceding factors make arbitrary estimates of the number of Chrismons needed to dress a tree little more than wild guesses. As a guide, the first tree at Ascension Church, a 14 foot red cedar *(Juniper virginiana)* required about

50 large and 70 small size Chrismons.

If a general rule is wanted, try this: For every three feet of height of a tree (trees between 12 and 21 feet in height), plan to use about 10 large (Chrismons A, E, J, and K, for example) designs, 3 medium (F, G, and M) size ornaments, and 12 small (B, C, D, and N) Chrismons. This estimate assumes that the tree will be in a corner against the walls. It does not include the miniatures in the Children's Corner.

A very full and compact table tree about 30 inches high can carry about 80 miniatures if it is decorated around its circumference.

REASONS FOR AND METHODS OF ADAPTING THE DIRECTIONS TO SPECIFIC NEEDS

While many individuals and groups will use these same patterns, the Chrismons that they will make will vary considerably. Some realize that they are in a new field and want to learn what is known before they experiment; they will copy each ornament exactly. Another person wants the unique; he will put at least one original idea on every Chrismon that he makes. For others, economy is most important; they will use only the least expensive materials.

In some groups, children make Chrismons; their leaders simplify the patterns so that the task is within the workers' abilities. In a few areas, certain supplies may not be obtainable; Chrismon makers there adjust the directions to what they can get. A home-owner has beautiful evergreens in the yard; she wants Chrismons that stand up under outdoor conditions.

* * *

It is expected that these instructions will be modified so that the Chrismons that are made are most meaningful to their makers and to those who see them, so that the trees proclaim the desired message. The directions for Chrismons E, L, M, Q, and R and the section on outdoor Chrismons on this page list and explain, in a practical way, how to make changes in materials and methods of construction. Read those directions to discover the various options that are open.

It is always best to use materials obtainable by the people who will see the tree. Only when a person puts what he has learned in church into practice in his personal life is his Christianity meaningful to himself and his neighbors. If materials are too exotic, the average person cannot take the idea home. This advice is particularly applicable to foreign users of the Chrismon idea. Remember the basic reasons back of the tree. Speak in a language that the people who hear can understand; let the message be one that the hearer can carry to someone else.

Natives of Tanganyika have made Chrismons. Even if an American or European saw them, however, they probably would not recognize them. But to those who made them, the Tanganyikan Chrismons mean the same as this country's Chrismons mean to citizens of this area. To most of the natives of Turuland, Chrismons made exactly like the ones in this book would not have any meaning. Wherever one is, whatever changes are made in the Chrismons, remember that their only importance lies in their meaning.

CHRISMONS FOR OUTDOOR USE

Chrismons for outdoor trees and floats in Christmas parades must be waterproof and unbreakable to avoid damage from rain, snow, and wind. This eliminates two frequently used items in Chrismon construction: Styrofoam glue and thin glass beads and balls. At the same time, Chrismons on outdoor trees are not examined too closely. Consequently, substitute construction methods need not allow for fine, detailed work.

Any beaded Chrismons that are made of gold metal or plastic beads or solid glass pearls can be used on outdoor trees safely. First, however, give them a protective coat of clear acrylic spray. Most Chrismon makers, though, would probably use less detailed work on outdoor trees, which are generally seen only from a distance.

Only the shape and color of the ornaments can be seen on most outdoor trees. Therefore, patterns for outdoor Chrismons should be the outline of the wanted design. (On beaded patterns, separate beads need not be indicated; instead make the edging lines straight.)

One-fourth inch outdoor plywood is the best base for outdoor Chrismons. Cut the designs out with a saber, jig, or band saw. (Less expensive grades of wood are satisfactory.) With waterproof paint (enamel), color the ornament the same white, gold, or combination of white and gold of the original design. The paint must cover all the surfaces and edges of the wood.

Gold paint should always be sprinkled heavily with gold glitter while the paint is still wet because gold paint is too dull to use alone. (Brush the paint on; sprayed-on paint dries too quickly for the glitter to adhere.) White paint can also be enriched by sprinkling it with white iris glitter. Or, sprinkle white paint very lightly with gold glitter to suggest the stretch mesh on the original designs.

Make hangers for plywood Chrismons of pieces of green twist tape. This tape-covered wire is available on rolls from garden shops and florists. Drill a hole in the top of the Chrismon. Run the end of a 12 inch piece of twist tape through the hole; twist the tape on itself to hold the end in place. The leftover tape is the hanger. Woven Chrismons for outdoor use should also have these tape hangers. Bare wires can cut into the bark of a tree.

While foam is not as durable as plywood, designs may also be cut from foam. This is the place for dynafoam or packing foam. Although they are not completely windproof, they are stronger than styrofoam. Wrap the glued-in styrofoam hanger atop the ornament with waterproof green plastic tape.

Plywood or foam outdoor ornaments may be wrapped with stretch mesh just as the original Chrismons are covered. Plywood may be further ornamented with white iris or gold waterproof sequins in various shapes. Glue them in place with household cement or epoxy glue. White or metallic gold polyethylene flowers are very effective decorations for outdoor use. Wire the flowers in holes drilled through the wood.

Because all the elements are waterproof, stranded wire wrapped with vinyl festooning can substitute for woven gold beads. Chrismon AA gives festooning wrapping directions.

For balls on outdoor trees, coat children's rubber or plastic balls with gold paint and glitter or use household cement to glue the glitter to the ball. Run a string or wire through the ball, from bottom to top, and then through a styrofoam cross on top. The string or wire wrapped with green tape becomes the hanger. Gold metal balls can be used in the same manner except that the string is tied around the top hanger before it is run through the cross.

WHICH CHRISMONS ARE EASIEST TO MAKE?

For those who desire it, an evaluation of the comparative ease of making Chrismons in the *Basic Series* is given below. Before using it, however, consider these points:

Workers use a wide variety of operations and skills to make various Chrismons. What may be easy for one person could be difficult for another. One experienced in weaving beads, for example, may find Chrismon V easier than Chrismon K.

Some estimates of the comparative ease of the work may not agree with the one below. On the average, however, the one below is more likely to be right because it is based on more Chrismon experience than any other could be. At the same time, another rating may not be "average."

The fact that few words are used to explain how to make a Chrismon does not necessarily mean that the ornament is easy to construct.

Most groups make Chrismons in the difficult group the first year. This listing, therefore, should not scare anyone off. But if someone must begin with a difficult one and has trouble as a consequence, do not let him or her throw up his or her hands and quit.

After skill is acquired on simple Chrismons, the difficult ones become less so. Easily discouraged people should not make it hard on themselves in the beginning. Take special care not to dishearten younger workers at the start.

Chrismon B is recommended as a starter for several reasons: It is easy to make; the materials are relatively easy to find at any time of the year; much can be learned about Christian symbolism in the work on this design alone; it starts a person thinking about carrying out his own ideas early in the project.

The easiest Chrismon to make is generally the one a person most wants to make.

To sum up: This evaluation is most helpful when it is used with common sense and with awareness of its limitations.

* * *

Very Easy to Make: B, C.

Easy to Make: D, E, G, L, N, Q2.

Average: A, F, J, M, P, Q3, R1, R2, R3, S, T, U, Y, AA, BB, CC, DD.

Somewhat Difficult: H, Q4, R4, V, W, X, Z, EE.

Difficult: Q1, FF.

OBTAINING MATERIALS AND SUPPLIES

In the first year of the Chrismon program, people used to write that the hardest part of carrying out the project was getting the materials to do the job. Letters with this complaint are now infrequent. One reason is that the resurgence of interest in arts and crafts has resulted in the opening of numerous stores (and sections of department stores) which sell many Chrismon supplies. Because of the growing number of Chrismon makers, some retail outlets even specialize in Chrismon supplies. In localities where such stores are found, obtaining materials presents no problems. Because Chrismon makers who do not have a craft outlet nearby may have trouble obtaining supplies, the following suggestions are offered.

While Chrismon materials are and have been generally available throughout the United States and Canada, not all of them are found in any one place at any one time. It may be necessary to shop around over a period of months or even years to obtain all the desired items. Some materials are seasonal and available only during the Christmas shopping season. While it is not easy to wait when interest in the Chrismon program is running high, it is sometimes the only course open. Immanuel Lutheran Church in Bluefield, West Virginia, found an excellent way to meet this problem. Materials were bought during the Christmas season. Then, during the following Lent, the people studied the meaning of the Chrismons and began to construct them.

Another supply difficulty is in finding the exact size bead or kind of decoration that is called for. The answer is substitution. Often the substitute is better than the original idea. A weave that combines 16 mm and 10 mm beads builds up to about the same size as a weave composed of 12 mm beads alone. See Chrismon J. A straight weave of 6 mm beads is about the same size as a single row of 16 mm beads.

* * *

Retail Sources:

In response to numerous requests for this information from Chrismon makers across the continent, the following firms that carry items needed in Chrismon construction are listed. These retailers make their Christmas merchandise available throughout the year. Many other stores would certainly be equally satisfactory, but this book lists only those that have been recommended by at least a dozen Chrismon makers who do not live in the city or town in which the business is located:

Piedmont Garden and Florist Supply (formerly Rufty's) 280 Furniture Drive, Salisbury, North Carolina 28144, has the widest assortment of Chrismon supplies of any firm known to Ascension Lutheran Church. They will send a free Chrismons materials price list to anyone who requests it.

MATERIALS USED IN THE CONSTRUCTION OF CHRISMONS

The following list covers materials used to make the designs in all four Chrismons books. A few supplies which are used on only one type of ornament are omitted because it would be necessary to go into directions for making the Chrismon to explain what is wanted. These items are described in the instructions for the Chrismon on which the material is used.

Not all of the following supplies are needed by every Chrismon maker. First, decide what ornaments are to be made. Then, get only those materials that are needed for those designs.

The letters in parentheses after the name of the material refer to the type of store at which that item may be found.

C—Craft or hobby shops; craft or hobby sections in 5 & 10, variety, and department stores.

D—Places which sell Christmas decorations.

F—Florists.

H—Hardware stores; hardware sections in 5 & 10, variety, and department stores.

N—Notions counters in 5 & 10, variety, and department stores.

* * *

Styrofoam (C, F): Light plastic foam sold in many sizes and shapes. The less expensive types have larger pores. Use only the finest grade with the smallest pores on any designs that require finely detailed carving with a knife. Florists often have finer grades when other sources do not. Use white only. White dynafoam and other insulating and packing foams may be substituted when the designs are cut out on a hot wire machine.

Artificial Flowers (C, F): White roses, daisies, lilies-of-the-valley, gladiolus, and selected other flowers in assorted sizes. Polyethylene flowers are the most durable.

Satin Balls (D): 3″ in diameter; white; in some cases, gold.

Clear Plastic Balls (D): 3″ in diameter.

Stemmed Balls (D, F): Shiny gold glass or plastic balls on stems; 12 mm to 50 mm.

Christmas Tree Balls (D): Shiny gold glass, plastic, or metal balls from 40 mm to 100 mm in size. While glass balls are least expensive, they are also least durable.

Sequins & Spangles (C, N): Assorted shapes and sizes from 5 mm to 20 mm. Use only gold, white, white iris, and crystal.

Gold Metal Beads (C, N): 3 mm to 16 mm round and oval; in packs.

Gold Plated Plastic Beads (C, N): 3 mm to 16 mm round & faceted; in packs.

Gold Glass Beads (D): 6 mm to 16 mm thin glass beads on strings.

Pearls (C, N): 2 mm to 16 mm round, oval, and baroque shapes. Simulated pearls in natural and/or white; in packs or on strings.

Crystal Beads (C, N): 5 mm to 16 mm glass or plastic transparent or transparent iridescent; round, faceted, and/or roundel baroque; in packs and on strings.

Teardrop Beads (C, N): Pearl, crystal, and red; in packs.

Seed Beads (C, N): Tiny gold, pearl, and clear glass; in packs or tubes.

Rocailles (C, N): Similar to seed but squarecut, short glass beads; in packs or tubes; gold, pearl, and clear.

Bugles (C, N): Like the rocailles above, but longer; gold, pearl, and/or clear in packs or tubes. Some Chrismons require unusually long or short bugles which may be available in packs or on strings.

Love Beads (C, N): Similar to rocailles but a bit larger with a large hole; gold, clear, and/or white, in packs.

Glitter (C, D, N): Little sparkling flakes in gold, white, white iris, and/or crystal; in packs or tubes.

Angel Hair (D): Cloud-like white fibers
or

Glass Wool (Pet Stores): Same type of fibers; used to filter aquarium water.

Sequin Material (C, N): 3″ wide gold or white iris foil-like material; by the yard.

Gold Festooning (C, D): Gold plastic, foil-like material, 2″ or 3″ wide; cut so that it is like a fringe; by the yard.

Stretch Mesh (C. D, F): Gold aluminum foil cut and stretched so that it looks like woven mesh; in a roll.

Gold-backed Paper (C, N, D): Shiny metallic gold on one side, silver on the other; in rolls.

Gold Foil (C, D): Heavy; metallic gold on one side, silver on the other; in sheets.

Fiberglass Sheets (C): White translucent fabric in sheets.

Transparent Plastic (C): Office supply stores, used to cover maps; farm supply stores, window glass substitute : Semi-rigid sheets of clear acetate, 10 mil thick.

Sequins-by-the-Yard (C, N): 5 mm gold, white, white iris, and crystal cup sequins woven on strings; by the yard.

Half-round Pearls on a Cord (C, N): 6 mm simulated pearls; by the yard.

Metallic Braids, Cords, & Edgings (C, N): Flat and round; gold thread, thread and sequin, paper, and/or foil; by the yard; 1/8″ to 1″ wide.

Lace (C, N): White thread laces from 1/4″ to 1″ wide; by the yard.

Gold Tinsel Garland (D): 1½″ to 3″ wide Christmas decoration; in long lengths.

Dipping Film, Wires (C): See page 3 of *Chrismons for Every Day*.

Cooking Crystals, Hardener, Foil (C): See page 3 of *Chrismons for Every Day*.

Sequin Pins (C, N): ½″ straight pins in packs; get gold if possible.

Straight Pins (N): 1 1/8″ long.

Sewing Cotton (N): White, green; on spools.

Gold Thread (C, N): Metallic gold; on cardboard or spools.

Pipe Cleaners (C, Drug Stores, Tobacconists): White cotton twisted on wires.

Chenille Stems (C, D, F, N): 12″ pipe cleaner type wires; white, metallic gold; green for hangers on miniatures.

Stranded (Cable) Wire (H): About 1/8″ diameter; by the foot.

Beading Wire (C, N): Thin wire on spools for weaving seed, rocaille, and bugle beads; get gold wire if possible.

is the sign for "gauge."

#30 Hair Wire (C, H, N): About twice as thick as beading wire; on spools or in coils; wire on spools is easier to handle; get gold colored wire if possible.

#18 or #20 Silver Colored Wire (C, H): In coils. Do not use aluminum wire; it is too soft to hold its shape on the designs that call for this size wire. Use silver colored wire for stringing pearls and transparent beads.

#18 or #20 Gold or Copper Colored Wire (C, H): Gold on spools; copper in coils. Do not use real copper unless it is hard; most copper wire in this size is soft drawn, too soft to hold its shape on the Chrismons. Use gold or copper colored wire for stringing gold beads.

#14 & #18 Green Florist Wire (C, F): Green enameled wire; use only the stiff wire in 18″ to 36″ lengths; green wire on spools is not satisfactory for Chrismon work.

Gold Paint (C, H): Pressurized spray can and/or brushing type paint.

White Paint (C, H): Pressurized spray can and/or brushing type paint.

Pearlized Spray (C, F): Paint in pressurized can; gives a pearly look to white items; used to enrich plastic flowers, white beads, and painted foams.

Crystal Clear Acrylic Spray (C, H): Clear plastic paint in pressurized can.

Gold Finish Metallic Leaf & Adhesive (C): See page 3 in *Chrismons for Every Day*.

White Glue (C, H, N): Milky white glue (Elmer's) which can be used on styrofoam; in squeeze bottles.

Clear Household Cement (C, H, N): Duco type glue sold in tubes.

Clear Epoxy Glue (C, H, N): Resin and catalyst in two tubes; must be mixed together just before use.

MEASUREMENTS

Bead sizes are given in millimeters. The comparison of the United States measurement and the metric systems on the drawing below is given in case a metric system ruler is not available.

COST OF SUPPLIES

In 1965, groups across the country gave these answers to the question, "How much did it cost?"

Tree Height	Cost	Comments
12′	$70.00	We should have had a 20′ tree for the Chrismons that we had; much material was left over.
15′	30.00	
15′	80.00	Much expensive material for use next year still on hand.
15′	60.00	
20′	100.00	No expense spared to have the best materials; most expensive construction methods used.
2 - 5′	30.00	Total cost for everything including the lights.

* * *

Because the cost of living has risen since 1965, present day prices are naturally higher than those shown above. These figures are given, however, to show that costs vary widely. The following factors govern one's expenses:

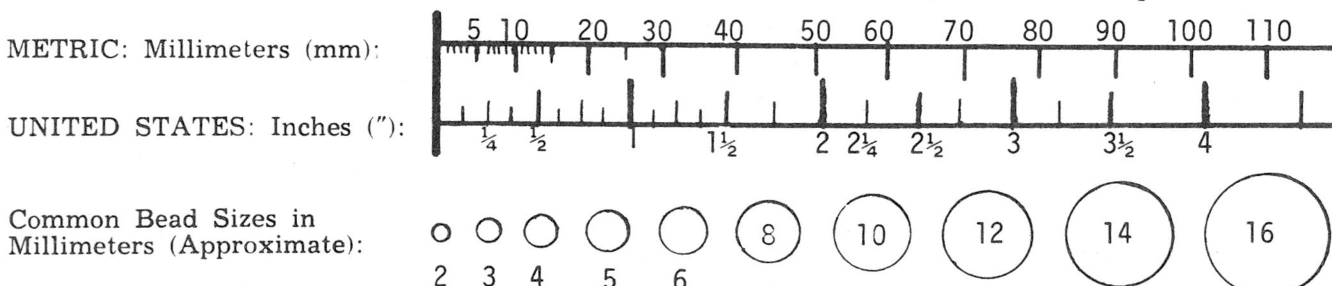

Kinds of Materials Used

Most Chrismons can be made from several materials. The more pearls, gold metal beads, sequins, and the like that are used—the higher the costs will be. To reduce costs, use more styrofoam, gold festooning, and glitter.

Shopping Know-How:

Costs can be kept down by buying materials when they are reduced (just after Christmas for some items) or at wholesale when possible. Do not overbuy; or, arrange for members of the group to buy the leftover materials to make Chrismons for personal use. Buy wisely. For example, one can pay from 5¢ to 50¢ for each miniature light on the tree. Generally the 50¢ lights are least suitable for Chrismon trees. Often multi-strand pearls are on sale on jewelry counters at prices less than wholesale costs.

Density of Tree Decorations:

This matter was explored under the "Number of Chrismons Needed" on page 10. More Chrismons and lights mean higher costs. Expenditures for overdecorating a tree are not justified, but many people do waste money in this manner.

* * *

How does a non-profit group finance a Chrismon tree? Here are some ideas that various groups have passed on:

1) Take the money from the group's treasury.
2) Ask for special gifts from "generous souls."
3) Let each Chrismon maker pay for the materials that he or she wants and uses.
4) Charge a flat fee to each person who wishes to work on the project.

These last two ideas may seem strange to one who is unacquainted with Chrismons. However, it is a fact that most people consider it a privilege to make Chrismons. If they do not think so before they start, they come to that conclusion when they see what they have done.

STORAGE OF CHRISMONS

Many Chrismons are used as inspirational decorations and teaching aids throughout the year. Still, the time comes when some of them are not needed for awhile; they must be packed away.

These ornaments must, first of all, be protected from breakage. Because Chrismons are more durable than they may appear to be, they do not break easily. If they are packed to lie flat and are held in that position, they will not be damaged. (Instructions are given for the storage of those Chrismon that cannot be packed in this manner in the directions for those particular designs. No Chrismons in the *Basic* or *Christian Year Series* are in this category except the Crown and the Sun of Righteousness. These Chrismons should be packed individually in pastry boxes as deep as the ornaments.)

Fully packed heavy suit boxes best meet Chrismon storage needs. The relatively shallow box can be filled without building up enough weight for the ornaments to crush one another.

Place each Chrismon to be packed in a transparent plastic bag. Put a layer of crumpled packing material across the bottom of the box. Then arrange a layer of Chrismons—all about the same thickness—on the packing. Continue to alternate layers of packing and Chrismons until the box is full. End with a layer of packing material. If the box is not full or if hollow spaces develop, fill them with packing material so that the Chrismons cannot shift about. Tie a cord around the box so that the lid cannot be dislodged. Chrismons stored in this manner can be shelved and/or carried right side up, upside down, and/or on end without damage.

* * *

The value of packing materials is determined by their ability to protect the Chrismons and their ease of use. The following listing presents the most desirable packing material first. Art foam (1/8 or 1/4 inch foam rubber); transparent plastic film (cleaner's bags without printing that may come off onto the Chrismons); the slightly waxed green paper used by florists; colored tissue paper; pieces of packing foam. Do NOT use white tissue paper; the paper itself may cause tarnish.

The only Chrismon materials that tarnish under normal conditions are the gold glitter, gold paint, and the wires. If one takes the trouble to find it, non-tarnishing glitter can be obtained. Gold leafing (metallic gold) over gold paint alleviates this problem. (See page 3 in *Chrismons for Every Day.*) Use of the packing materials suggested above will help to prevent tarnish in all except certain areas close to some chemical plants. Airtight packing will help to retard tarnish in those places.

The best protection against tarnish, however, is a coating of clear plastic spray on the Chrismon after it is constructed. Such coatings cannot be applied to styrofoam unless it has been treated to a coating of glue. (See page 4 in *Chrismons for Every Day.*)

LIGHTS ON CHRISMON TREES

Lights are not necessary on Chrismon trees; some groups use them, some do not. If lights are wanted, however, the strings of clear or white miniature bulbs that have come on the market during the past 15 years are strongly recommended. Each light is about one-third the size of a peanut; 10 to 100 screw-in or push-in bulbs are on each string. Even if one or more bulbs burn out, the other bulbs remain lighted. Spare bulbs are available.

When the lights are strung around the tree, especially at the top, some will shine through the branches. When a viewer moves his or her head, the effect is of twinkling starlight because the filament in the light is so small that even a twig can hide it momentarily. This method of lighting the tree realizes the aim that Martin Luther was reputed to have had in his invention of the Christmas tree.

* * *

Miniature lights are now widely available. If a string has a blinking bulb, replace the blinker with a plain bulb. A number of miniature strings have novelty holders (flowers, animals, Santas, angels) and colors. Use only the most simple green holders on green wires and only white or clear bulbs. Everyone who speaks of it believes that colored lights would detract greatly from the effectiveness of the tree.

Because miniature bulbs are so tiny, more of them than regular Christmas tree bulbs are needed to light the tree well. However, do not use too many lights. Their brilliance could keep viewers from seeing the Chrismons on the tree. When visitors are welcomed to see the Chrismon tree at Ascension Church, those who present the tree frequently turn the tree lights off during parts of the explanation. A 15 foot tree can use about five strings of 50 lights each or 250 lights.

Holy Trinity Lutheran Church in West Allis, Wisconsin, places a light on its tree for each family in the parish. Some congregations put a light on the tree for each member. Certainly this practice can remind each of us of our Lord's commission to let our "light shine before all men." (Matthew 5:16.) Thus others, through us, can see the One Who said, "I am the light of the world." (John 8:12.)

GENERAL CONSTRUCTION TECHNIQUES FOR CHRISMONS

The following procedures must be used over and over again in making various Chrismons. Rather than explain them every time that they are used, the directions for these operations are given here.

HANGERS FOR CHRISMONS

Decoration of a Chrismon tree is not merely a matter of ornamenting a tree; it is a proclamation of the Christ. The tree must speak clearly so that everyone can understand. Others can comprehend what is said only when the Chrismons are hung so that anyone who looks at them can "read" them. The correct side must always face out, and the ornament should be on a plane with and parallel to the surface of the tree. Since this is difficult to do with ordinary ornament hangers, the following kinds of hangers are recommended for use.

FIGURE 1

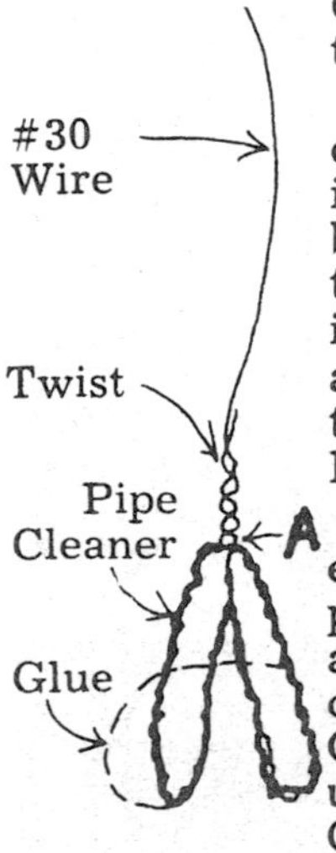

Styrofoam Hanger:

Use this hanger atop any Chrismon that has styrofoam at the top.

Bend a 1¼ inch piece of pipe cleaner at its center. Bend a 12 inch piece of #30 wire over the bend in the pipe cleaner so that the bend of the #30 wire is one inch from the end. Twist the one and eleven inch ends together next to the pipe cleaner end, A on Figure 1 at the left.

Cover the base of both cleaner ends with white glue. Push the pipe cleaner ends into the foam atop the Chrismon until the pipe cleaner bend is level with the Chrismon top. Do not leave an ugly protusion atop the ornament. Only the #30 wire should show.

To keep the hanger wire from tangling, wrap it into a coil. Place a one-half to one-fourth inch round form (pen, pencil, or dowel) next to A on Figure 1. Wrap the leftover #30 wire tightly around the round form. Slip the form out; the #30 wire holds its curl neatly until it is straightened to hang the ornament on the tree.

The long wire enables the Chrismon to hang on the tree where it is wanted. Furthermore, an ornament on such a wire hangs where it is placed instead of twisting about uncontrollably.

Woven Bead Hanger:

When the top of a Chrismon ends in beads woven on #30 wire, plan to have about 12 inches of leftover wire at the end of the weave. Twist two leftover weaving wires tightly together. Cut off the shorter one. The remaining wire is the hanger. Curl it on a round jig to keep it from tangling as explained above.

Top Wire Hanger:

When the top beads of a Chrismon are on a heavy wire (20 gauge or larger), bend the end of a 12 inch piece of #30 wire over the heavy wire. Twist the one and eleven inch ends of the #30 wire tightly together to hold at the heavy wire. Curl the leftover wire on a round jig. This is one time when it is advisable to use green enameled #30 wire; the green will not show against the woven beads or against an evergreen tree.

METHODS OF CUTTING STYROFOAM

The beginning Chrismon maker often has great difficulty in cutting styrofoam. This problem is hárd to understand because, done properly, cutting foam is quite easy. However, two practices can make this simple task difficult for anyone: Trying to do the work too quickly and using the wrong tools.

Because styrofoam is soft and easily broken and cut, some beginners seem to think that they can zip through the job any way they choose. They are in trouble at once! Does one not have to use the proper tools and a certain sawing motion to cut a smooth slice of bread or a thin, even slice of ham? Much the same motion and care is needed to cut styrofoam with a knife.

After all, cutting out the styrofoam, even when it is done slowly, takes little time compared to most other jobs necessary to make a Chrismon. So, take time to carefully trace and cut out the pattern for the foam. Use care in transferring the pattern to the foam. When the cut is made by hand, SAW; do not chop or push.

* * *

The following tools will cut styrofoam. Not all of them are needed. In fact, all the Chrismons can be cut out with only one tool. However, the proper selection of tools results in the most easily made and durable Chrismons. Note especially that different kinds of patterns must be made for the various cutting tools.

Hot Wire Cutting Machine:

Florists and display workers cut styrofoam with a machine which melts the plastic with a hot wire. Such an apparatus is the easiest cutting tool to use. It also gives the smoothest edge and actually adds strength to the foam. (When the melted foam solidifies, it is harder than it was before it was cut.)

While the hot wire machine is the easiest cutting tool, it can be employed only to make cuts straight through the full thickness of the foam. Thus, it will not make the cuts that shape the front of the triangle on Chrismon T. On the other hand, the outline of this Chrismon should be cut on a hot wire machine because of the narrowness of parts of the design. The extra strength given to the styrofoam by the machine is needed to make the ornament durable.

Hot wire cutters are available from craft and hobby shops and florists. Prices start at $1.50 for a battery operated hand tool and go up to $25.00 for an elaborate, AC electric table model. Many individuals have built their own machines with heat resistant wire and a doorbell transformer. Because the wire loses heat if it burns too long, a machine with a handy cut-off switch is most convenient. If a less expensive plug-in model without a switch is used, an extension cord with a switch on it works well.

Patterns for Chrismons to be cut out on a hot wire machine should be made of light cardboard about the weight of a manila folder. Because the wire melts some foam under the cardboard, the pattern must be about 1/16 inch larger on every cutting line than the drawing in the instructions. Thus, the cut out design becomes the same size as the original pattern.

Place the cardboard pattern on the styrofoam. Run sequin pins through the cardboard into the styrofoam to hold the pattern in place. Cut out the design by running the styrofoam slowly and steadily through the hot wire while the pattern edge gently rides along the wire. Whenever the pattern is against the wire, the foam must be kept in motion to avoid burning a depression in the outline of the design.

Little practice is needed to get the "feel" of the hot wire machine. Even six-year-old children can learn to operate it with supervision. It is not only the best tool for cutting styrofoam but is also the only tool that yields a good edge on many packing foams.

When using the hot wire machine, be sure to keep the foam flat on the cutting table. Curves and straight lines are cut in one continuous move of the pattern against the wire. To cut an inner corner, move the pattern along one side to the corner. Pause a fraction of a second at the corner; then move smoothly out of the corner along the opposite side of the angle. Do not, however, move the cardboard around an outside corner. When this is done, the wire burns the edge and rounds the corner instead of making a sharp angle. Rather, continue the cut beyond the corner. Cut the other side of the corner in another move of the foam.

Jig Saw, Band Saw, Saber Saw in a Stand—all with metal cutting blades:

Cardboard patterns for use with these tools should be about 1/16 inch smaller than the diagrams in the books. Place the patterns atop the styrofoam. With a pencil, trace around the pattern on the styrofoam. Then follow the pencil lines to cut out the designs. If more than one Chrismon in a design is wanted, several layers of foam may be stacked atop one another and cut out by the one pattern on the top piece. Use sequin or straight pins to hold the foam layers together. Men and boys do this work well.

Very Sharp Wood-Carving Hobby Knives:

These may be bought in hobby and craft shops and some hardware and variety stores. X-acto is a well-known trade name. Various blades are available for different types of cuts. These knives cut styrofoam easily because they are sharp. When they become dull, and they will, they "rag" the foam. They MUST be kept sharp. Macon Methodist Church in Tecumseh, Michigan, suggests whetting a knife on paraffin for a smoother cut.

Make cardboard patterns and trace them onto the styrofoam as explained for the jig saw cuts above. Cut out the design with a sawing motion.

While these knives can make all the Chrismons in any of the books, cutting out the designs on electric saws or a hot wire machine is easier and quicker. Hot wire machine cuts are definitely better because of their added strength.

On the other hand, this type of knife is necessary if the most elaborately carved Chrismons, "Angels and Archangels," are made. It is also the best tool for the easy touch up work that cannot be done on a hot wire machine such as the surface carving on the triangle of Chrismon T. If one wants to develop skill in carving styrofoam, it is well to use an X-acto knife for such tasks from the beginning. The "Angel" directions in the *Advanced Series* give more complete information on this procedure.

Paring Knife with Serrated (Saw-like) Edge:

This is the least expensive and the most readily available tool. Every Chrismon in this book can be cut out with it, and every original Chrismon was first made with it. Agreed, this is the slowest and most tedious method. Nevertheless, it puts the Chrismons within the reach of anyone who wants to make them.

Large knives with serrated edges cannot do this job satisfactorily; the blade is too large to get into small spaces. Nor can kitchen knives without serrated edges be used to cut styrofoam; the edges are not sharp enough.

To use a serrated paring knife, make the pattern and trace it onto the styrofoam as directed for the jig saw pattern above. SAW the design out with the serrated edge of the knife. Do not try to cut it out; saw! If the job is done slowly and easily, it is within the abilities of workers of average manual dexterity. This tool is not suitable for cutting packing foams.

Single Edged Razor Blade:

This tool can be used like an X-acto knife except on Chrismons with small cutouts. Chrismon T and the home size of Chrismon A are in this category.

Note: Smooth out little irregularities in styrofoam by pushing them in with the fingers or a knife blade. Use another piece of styrofoam to sand styrofoam smooth.

DECORATIVE FINISHES FOR STYROFOAM

While styrofoam can be used in its natural state, some surface decoration is generally applied. Plain foam often appears on miniatures. Directions for almost all other Chrismons, however, suggest specific finishes. One should not feel obliged to follow the written suggestions. Rather, be free to alter the ornamentation to whatever procedure is wanted.

Light or Heavy Coating of Glitter:

A sprinkling of white or gold glitter is the easiest and least costly foam decoration to use.

Several types of "white" glitter are available: "Crystal" glitter has an attractive sheen and a light, airy appearance; "white iris" glitter echoes the rainbow in its reflections; "white" glitter, the least desirable, looks chalky and adds little to the appearance of the foam. A light sprinkling of a white glitter is not recommended; the effect is so minimal that it is not worth the trouble. Therefore, use white glitters only in heavy or medium coats.

When tiny flakes of gold glitter are lightly sprinkled on white foam, the effect is similar to covering styrofoam with stretch mesh. On the other hand, when gold glitter is applied heavily, the white foam is converted to glittering gold, and the nature of the design is altered. One should be certain that this change is wanted before making it. This heavy gold coating is advisable when styrofoam substitutes for a solid gold design such as a weave of gold beads. The gold glitter makes it possible to use styrofoam on an originally beaded design without changing the balance of the original Chrismon.

* * *

To apply a light sprinkling of glitter to foam, brush white glue lightly over the plastic. Then sprinkle glitter on the foam; let it dry.

When a heavy coat of glitter that covers the foam completely is wanted, paint the foam solidly with white glue. Before it begins to "crawl," sprinkle the glue heavily with glitter. Since the glue will crawl before most Chrismons are covered, the glittering of the design must be done in sections. Trying to cover the design with one painting of the glue results in white spots of foam showing through the gold.

An even coat of glitter through which a bit of styrofoam shows is obtained by painting the design with a mixture of two-thirds glue to one-third water. Gold or white glitter is then sprinkled on the design. If the glue mixture is put into a bowl, miniatures can be quickly dipped and covered with glitter.

Covering Styrofoam with Stretch Mesh (Expansion Foil):

If the mesh is not stretched, gently pull it out to its expanded size. Keep the gold side of the foil out, the silver against the styrofoam. To cover any shape except a circle (see page 24 for circle directions), place the mesh on the foam design. Cut a piece of mesh that extends one inch beyond each edge of the ornament. See Figure 2 on this page below. Hold the mesh atop the foam; cut the foil mesh to each point above each inner corner of the Chrismon. See the heavy A lines on Figure 2.

Wrap the mesh smoothly and firmly over each arm of the design. Cut off any mesh that would lap back over the face of the design. If the foil was not stretched too tightly before it was cut, it can be eased over bare spots of foam.

FIGURE 2

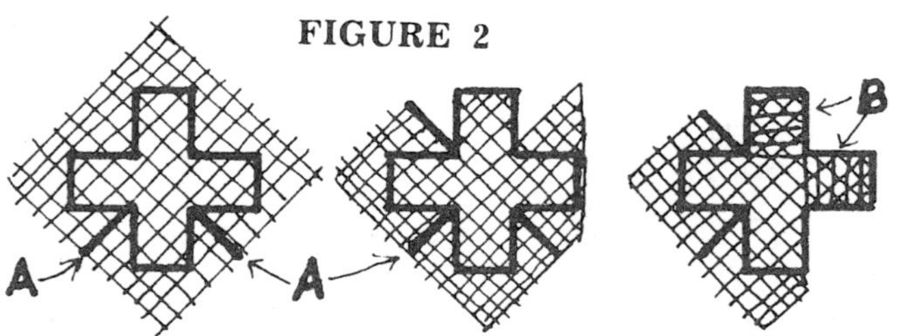

Anchor the mesh in place with white thread. Knot a circle of thread around the end of an arm; spiral the thread to the center of the ornament and then out to the end of another arm. See B on Figure 2. Continue this procedure until all the mesh is anchored. If the thread is wrapped smoothly, it can be seen only when one is quite close to the Chrismon. However, it does much to prolong the life of the ornament.

Stretch Mesh Substitutes:

Sometimes, stretch mesh is difficult to find. The following may be substituted:

A type of metallic gold mesh, similar to a woven lace, can be used instead of stretch mesh on Chrismon E. Because this material must be sewn in place, it cannot be used on designs like crosses when cuts must be made to the center.

Ribbon-like sequin material with round holes punched out can be applied with the stretch mesh procedure. The effect of an ornament decorated with this material, however, is not as delicate.

Smooth Pearlized or Gold Finish:

Rough styrofoam can be smoothed by applying white glue which is sanded after it is dry. This new surface may be given a white pearlized or shiny gold leaf finish. While these procedures require more time than those listed above, the resulting surface is the finest of all the finishes. "Finishing the Styrofoam" on page 31 of *Chrismons for Every Day* shows how to apply the pearlized surface. Directions for the head of the fish on page 66 under Chrismon FF in this book explain the gold leaf finish.

A delicate, carved effect can be given styrofoam by gluing coarse lace to the surface of smoothed foam. See page 36 in *Chrismons for Every Day* for instructions in this procedure.

Attaching Sequins and Flowers to Foams:

The directions often suggest placing sequins and/or flowers on styrofoam Chrismons. While pinning a sequin to the foam seems to hold it, the pin alone is not durable. For a decoration that lasts, white glue must first be placed on the foam where the pin is to enter. Let it dry.

Flowers on wire stems may be glued to the foam by treating the stem in the same manner as the pin above. Since plastic, however, does not hold to white glue well, flowers of this material must be taken apart. After a 3 to 5 mm pearl is run on a straight pin, the petals and cup are also run onto the pin. Glue the pin to the foam as directed for the sequin pin above.

WEAVING BEADS ON WIRES

Selection of Beads:

The first beaded Chrismons were made of thin gold glass beads on nine foot strings. Even in bulk, they are light and inexpensive. Moreover, these beads have holes large enough to carry the heavy wires that are needed to support larger Chrismons. Pipe cleaners and 14 gauge wires can pass through them easily.

These glass beads also have disadvantages: They are less durable than most beads. Because of their thin glass walls, they are more difficult to weave tightly; however, a ten year old child can weave them successfully. Thin glass beads are made only in 6 mm and larger sizes.

* * *

Gold metal beads can be substituted for many gold glass beads. When 3 mm to 5 mm and 3 x 6 mm beads are called for, gold metal, the only materials in which these sizes are made, must be used. Metal beads, the most durable of all beads, are also available in all the other needed sizes. Furthermore, they are the easiest beads to weave because, regardless of the pressure, they will not break. Note: Designs woven of metal or the plastic beads below will be smaller than Chrismons made of the same size glass beads. The necks on the glass beads add to the weaving size of the beads.

Still, metal beads have disadvantages: They are the most expensive and heaviest beads to use. If all the Chrismons to decorate a tree are of metal beads, no gold ornaments could hang on tiny twigs; all the designs would be too heavy. Holes in metal beads are often too small for the heavy wires that support some Chrismons. While some Chrismon makers drill each bead to enlarge the holes, this tedious process also often cracks the gold plating of the beads.

* * *

Gold plated plastic beads have recently come on the market. (Durlon is one trade name.) They are made in round and faceted shapes. In some ways, these beads are the ideal selection for Chrismon use. Although they are a little heavier than thin glass beads, they are much lighter than metal beads. Their holes are about as large as glass beads, and their durability almost equals that of metal beads. Although plastic beads are more expensive than glass, they are less costly than metal ones. The chief disadvantage of these gold plated plastic beads is that they are not available in as wide a range of sizes as the metal and glass beads.

* * *

Although simulated pearls are not quite as durable as metal, they withstand all the pressure needed to make Chrismons. Sometimes, plastic pearls, lighter than covered glass beads, are available.

Small seed, rocaille, and bugle beads are more easily broken than larger beads. However, they are quite durable when they are strung. Breakage in stringing them can be reduced by using beading instead of #30 wire. When #20 wires must be used, love beads and/or oversize bugles with large holes can be used.

Weaving Wires:

Remember that higher gauge numbers refer

to smaller size wires. Because beading wire is more flexible than #30 wire, it may be easier to use with gold glass beads. But it is not strong enough to support most weaves of such beads.

Whenever possible, use gold colored wire with gold beads and silver colored wire for pearls or crystal beads. Use green wire for hangers or as supports. Do not attempt to substitute wires on coils or spools for stiff wires that come in straight lengths or stiff for coiled wire. Their characteristics are quite different.

Weaving Hints:

Keeping the wires smooth and pulling them tight are the two most important factors in weaving. If a kink develops in a wire, unwind it. Jerking or pulling a kink out weakens the wire. Learn from the beginning to keep weaving wires smooth. When a wire needs smoothing, pull it between a thumb and a pencil or similar object.

Washing the hands just before weaving removes skin oils that make the wires slippery. Do not use hand lotion before weaving. Even though it is a non-greasy type, it lubricates the wires so that a tight weave is impossible. Work on a dark surface; it is easier on the eyes.

It is simpler to learn to weave pearl, metal, or plastic beads than thin glass ones. Wires can be pulled tighter without breaking the beads. When learning to weave thin glass beads, one MUST break some beads. Unless beads are broken, the weaver never learns to pull wires tightly enough for the weave to hold its shape.

After weaving the Alpha and Omegas below, weave Chrismon J. The directions for that design include basic weaving procedures which are not repeated elsewhere in this book.

ALPHA AND OMEGA

(These letters hang on Chrismons A, E, J, and N.)

The first, Alpha (A, a), and the last, Omega (Ω, ω), letters of the Greek alphabet are often used in Christian art to suggest, as they do in the Bible, the divinity of our Lord. (Isaiah 44:6; Revelation 1:8, 22:13.) Early church usage combined the letters with the cross and later with the Chi Rho and other Christian symbols.

* * *

Alpha: Place a bead 4 inches from one end of a 12 inch piece of #30 wire. Hold the wire ends slightly apart between the thumb and forefinger about one-half inch from the bead; turn the bead so that the wires twist on themselves next to the bead. See the bead on Figure 3 on this page. (Note: Figure 3 shows the beads loosely strung so that the wires can be seen clearly. The actual weave must be tight; twists must be next to the beads.) String two more beads over both wire ends. Bead another wire like the first.

String two beads on the long wire of one leg. (Detail 1 of Figure 3.) Run the long wire from the other leg through these same two beads from the opposite directions. (Detail 2.) Pull the crossed over wires tight; bend them upward.

String two beads over both wires at each side. (Detail 3.) Then run both long wires through another bead. (Detail 4.) Pull the long wires tight. Rerun each long wire through the top bead in the same directions that the wires first went through the bead. This anchors the top bead on the wires to hold the letter together; it is called a "straight line anchor." (If a pattern does not show a top bead through which both wires run, twist the wires together to hold at the top.) With diagonal pliers, cut off the short wires. Attach the Alpha to the Chrismon with the long leftover wires.

* * *

Omega: Begin the Omega as the Alpha was begun, but, instead of adding two pearls on each leg, string seven on each side. Cut off the short wire on each side. Cross over the long wires in another bead. (Detail 5.) Pull the wires to the top of the bead; twist them to hold tightly together. Shape the Omega to the pattern.

* * *

Omega, Lower Case: String the first beads of the Omega in the same way as the Alpha except to put four beads over both wires on each leg. Run all the wires through three beads. (Detail 6.) Cut the short wires off. Straight line anchor the long wires on the top bead. Shape the legs of the Omega to the pattern.

* * *

Cross Topped Omega: Follow the directions for the lower case Omega, but run only two beads on all the wires. On one long wire, string two beads, B and C on Detail 7. Turn the second bead, C, so that its hole is at a right angle to the hole of bead B. Run the wire back through bead B. Pull the wires tight; adjust them so that about one-eighth of an inch slack is in the wires between beads B and C. Hold the wire at D and the bottom of the Omega firmly in one hand. With the other hand, turn bead C so that the wires between B and C twist on themselves. Make a like extension on the other long wire.

String two more beads on all the wires to complete the upright of the cross. Straight line anchor the top bead on the long wires. Cut off the two short wires. A cross may be put atop the Alpha in the same manner.

FIGURE 3

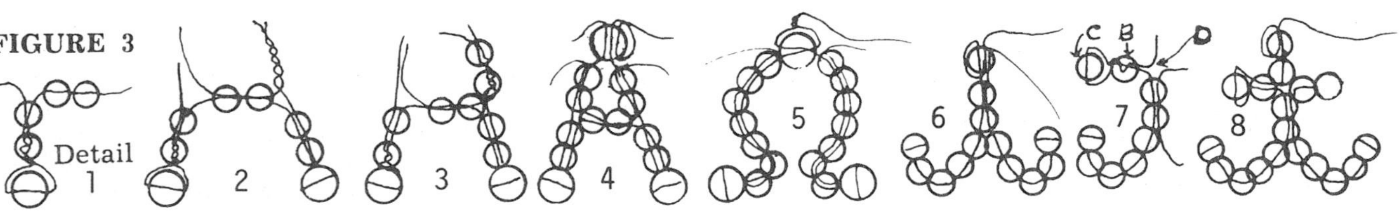

IV Patterns, Directions, & Interpretations of The Symbols

A. CHI RHO with ALPHA & OMEGA

(Illustrated on the back cover.)

The most widely known Chrismon is a combination of the first two letters of the Greek word for Christ, *Christos (XPISTOS)*, The Chi Rho (XP) was widely used by the early church. In that day, the shame and pain of the cross was too immediate for most people to use the sign of the cross openly.

This is the emblem, legend says, that Constantine saw in the sky with the cross and the words, "In this sign, conquer." So, continues the story, the Roman Caesar fought the definitive battle for Rome in 312 A.D. under this sign for the Christ. It is a fact that Constanstine later placed the Chi Rho atop his labarum, the standard carried before him, to signify that his was an empire under the Christ, a Christian people. He defended the church against further persecution, became a Christian himself, and abolished the cross as a form of execution because his Lord had died on it. Since then, use of this monogram has also implied the triumph of Christianity.

FIGURE 4

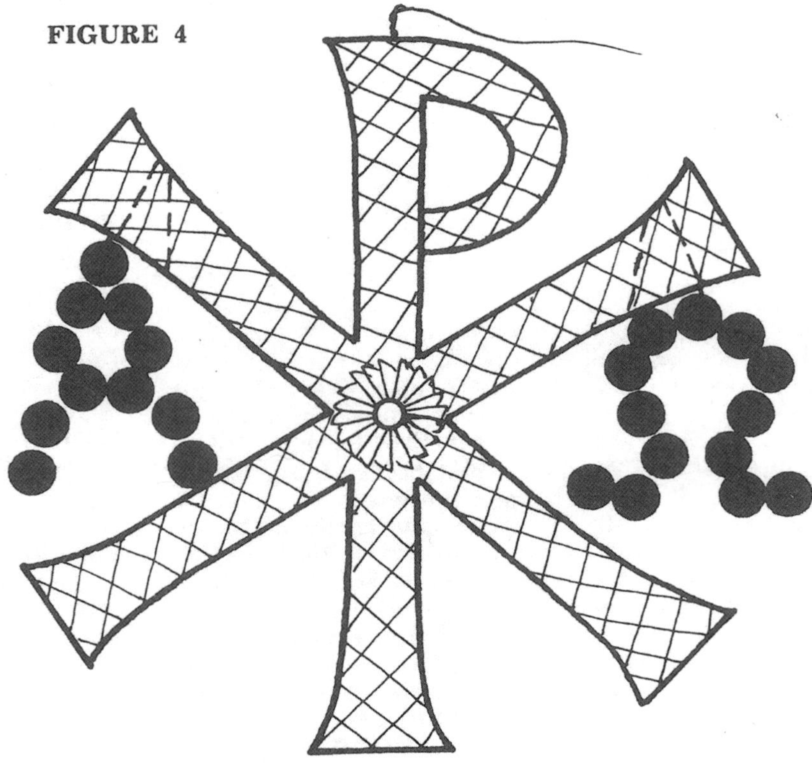

Another interpretation of the Chi Rho is based on the Latin phrase, *Christus Rex*, Christ the King. As early as the fourth century, the Alpha and Omega were added to the emblem to symbolize the divinity of Christ Jesus.

Sometimes people say, "Let's take the X out of Christmas!" This X which is the Greek Chi stood for Christ over a thousand years before the English language, of which the word *Christ* is a part, even began to develop.

Materials: ½" white styrofoam; gold stretch mesh; 6 mm gold beads; #30 wire; styrofoam hanger; ornamental gold sequin if desired; styrofoam glue; white thread.

Directions:

Cut out the Chi Rho by the colored background pattern on page 22 from one-half inch thick white styrofoam. Cover the monogram with gold stretch mesh; anchor the mesh with white thread.

Make the Alpha and Omega of 6 mm gold glass or metal beads on #30 hair wire. (See page 20.) Attach the letters to the arms of the Chi (X) by running the wire at the top of the letters through the styrofoam at the proper point on the X. See the dotted line over the Omega. Styrofoam glue at the entry and exit points of the #30 wire anchors the letters in place. Glue a styrofoam hanger at the top of the upright of the Rho (P).

A 20 to 24 mm gold sequin or flower may be placed at the center of the XP. Run the pin through a 5 mm pearl, the sequin, and into the styrofoam; or run the pin through a gold rocaille, a 5 mm gold cup sequin, and the ornamental sequin before gluing it into the Chi Rho. Suitable designs include a rose (Nativity), a butterfly (Resurrection), and a sunburst. Use the symbol that means what YOU want to say: The Savior is born! The Christ is risen! Christ, the Sun of Righteousness, is the Sun of my life!

Half (Home) Size Chrismon:

Use the pattern on Figure 4 above to cut the half size Chi Rho from one-half inch styrofoam. The home size design is made in the same way as the full size Chrismon except: 1) Fewer beads are used in the Alpha and Omega. Count them on the pattern. 2) The center sequin is smaller, 20 to 14 mm in size.

B. CORNERSTONE

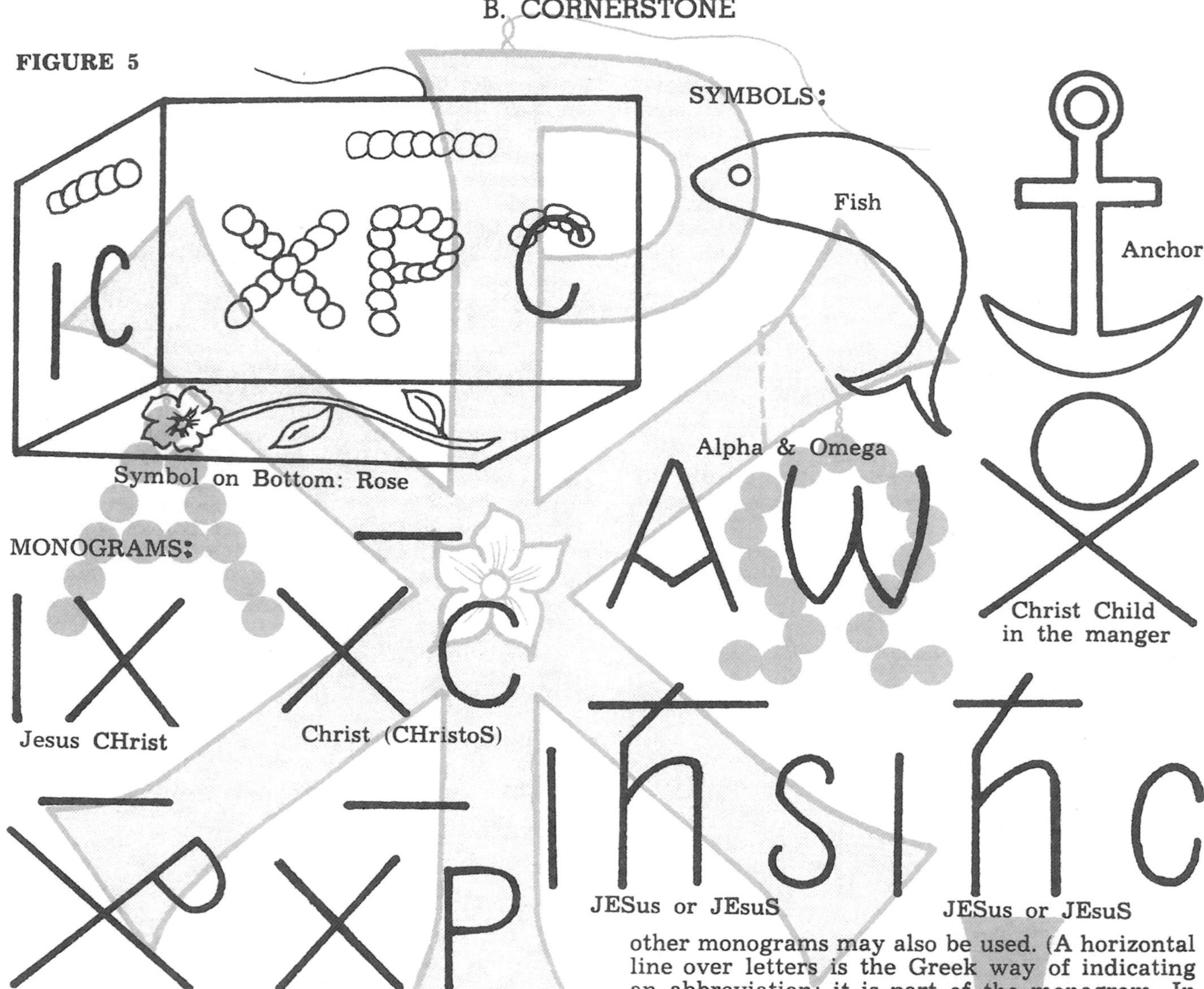

(Photograph on page 21.)

"The very stone which the builders rejected has become the head of the corner." Mark 12:10.

". . . . . Christ Jesus himself being the chief cornerstone." Ephesians 2:20.

Materials: 2" white styrofoam; crystal, white, or white iris glitter; 5 mm gold sequins-by-the-yard or 1/8" to 1/4" gold cord; white glue; sequin pins; assorted gold and/or white spangles, beads, foil, cords, braids, etc.

Directions:

From two inch thick white styrofoam, cut blocks 2 by 1 3/4 by 2 3/4 inches. The 2 3/4 by 2 inch faces are the top and bottom of the cornerstone.

With a pencil draw a monogram of our Lord on each of the side faces of the block. Sample monogram patterns are on Figure 5 above, but other monograms may also be used. (A horizontal line over letters is the Greek way of indicating an abbreviation; it is part of the monogram. In Greek, C is an older form of S; their meanings are the same. Some monograms are of the first and last letters of the name or title; some are the first two or three letters; others are the first two and the last letters.)

Draw the monograms on the styrofoam as they are shown on the pattern; the thread that holds the sequins together or the center of the cord follows the pattern lines. Place and glue gold cord or sequins-by-the-yard on the lines to make the letters. Pin the ends of the sequin or cord lengths to hold them in place until the glue is dry.

Insert and glue a styrofoam hanger into the center of the top. Draw guide lines for a symbol for our Lord on the bottom of the cornerstone and, if desired, another on the top. (A cornerstone that hangs above eye-level on a tree does not require a symbol on its top.) Several symbols are shown on the Figure above. Some, the Alpha and Omega and the fish, for example, can be made of 5 mm gold sequins-by-the-yard. Fancy flower and leaf sequins with gold bugles on #30 wire make a rose or a daisy. Other symbols that may be made from fancy sequins are eleven small and one large star with a sun and moon, twelve stars of equal size (twelve tribes or apostles), twelve fish with one large fish, and a large sunburst for the Sun of Righteousness. Gold foil can be cut to the shape of various crosses such as the anchor cross on Figure 5. Beaded wires may be shaped to form a shepherd's crook or a crown. Wheat, grapes, or symbols of our Lord's passion may also be worked out of varied materials. Pin and glue the sequins and/or beads in place to make the desired symbols.

Finally, apply a thin coat of white, white iris, or crystal glitter to those sections of the cornerstone that are left bare. Use a mixture of one-half to two-thirds glue diluted with water. Brush the glue mixture on the corners, edges, and other blank spaces of the surfaces of the cornerstone, which is held by the hanger. Sprinkle the wet surfaces with white or crystal glitter. Let it dry thoroughly. This easy Chrismon can be made in many variations.

C. CROSS ATOP ORB

(Photograph on the back cover.)

Artists often depict our Lord holding an orb, the world and the heavens around it, topped with a cross to symbolize His dominion over the earth.

Materials: ½" white styrofoam; gold glitter; 40 to 80 mm gold Christmas tree or stemmed (preferable) ball; styrofoam hanger; white glue.

Directions:

Cut the cross from one-half inch styrofoam by the colored background pattern on page 22.

Remove the stem from a gold stemmed ball (or the metal cap from a tree ball). Push the bottom of the cross over the neck of the ball; turn the cross and ball so that the neck cuts into the cross until the base of the cross rests on the ball; separate them. Coat the base of the cross with white glue; fit the ball and cross together. (When a neck of a tree ball is large, half inch foam will not cover it; in such cases, use one inch thick styrofoam.) Glue a styrofoam hanger to the top of the cross.

Apply a thin line of white glue to the corner edges of the cross; sprinkle the wet glue heavily with gold glitter. Let it dry thoroughly.

Since this Chrismon may be made in several sizes, patterns to fit various balls are given.

D. IOTA CHI (IX)

(Photographs on the front cover and this page at the left.)

The Iota (I), is the first letter of our Lord's given name Jesus in Greek. This name means "the promised one." The Chi (X) is the first letter of His Greek title Christ. The Greek word for Christ, *Christos (XPISTOS)*, is the translation of the Hebrew "Messiah", which means "the one anointed by God." When these two letters are superimposed, they become our Savior's cipher, the symbolic interweaving of initials that some people call a star. This Chrismon is easy for children to understand.

Materials: Assorted gold glass or metal beads from 6 to 16 mm; gold seed beads; 5 mm gold sequins; #30 hair wire. This ornament may also be made entirely in pearls. The size and number of beads that are used determine the diameter of the finished Chrismon, which may vary from 2½" to 4½". Because this is a good "filler" Chrismon on the tree, it is suggested that several be made in different sizes and of various beads. Use up odds and ends of leftover beads to work out a pleasing pattern from the available beads. Note that the patterns and photographs show different sizes and numbers of beads in the arms.

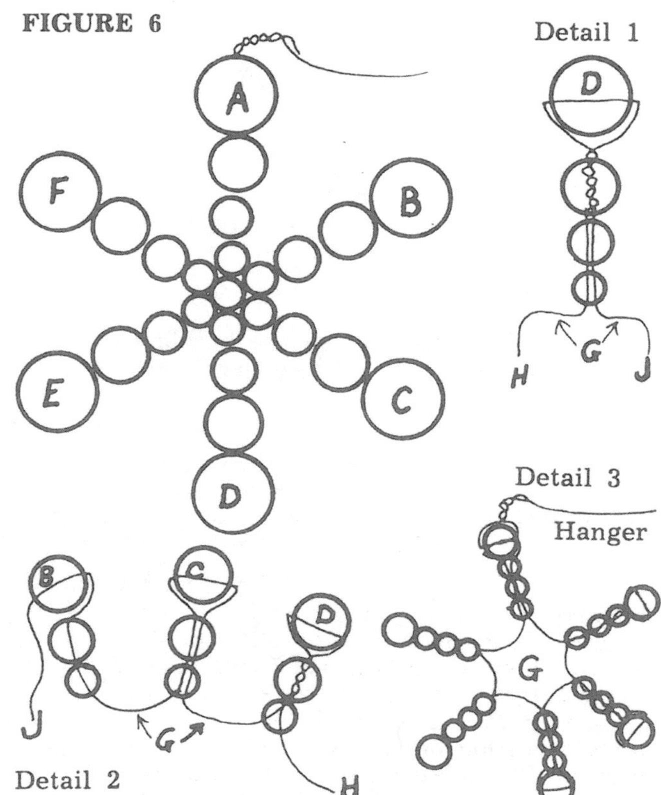

Directions:

Start the weave of this design at point D on Figure 6 on page 23. Place a large bead in the middle of a 30 inch length of #30 wire. Twist the wires together to hold the bead in place. String the remainder of the beads that compose one arm on both strands of wire. Bend the wires to anchor them at the end of the arm. See Detail 1 of Figure 6.

String the beads of arm C on wire J. Start at the center bead and go to the end bead. After the end bead, run the wire back through the other beads of the arm in reverse order to the center. Adjust the wire and beads so that the free wire between arms D and C is about ¾ inch long. Hold the wires (in and out of the arm) at point G while twisting the end bead to anchor it in place. See Detail 2. String arm B in the same manner as C; anchor arm B in place.

String arms E and F on wire H in the same way as arms B and C were strung. Bring wires J and H together; string the beads of arm A, except the end bead, over both wires. Separate the wires; run each wire through the end bead from opposite sides. Take the wires to the top of the end bead; twist them together to make a hanger. The design now looks like Detail 3.

Fold the arms diagonally over the spaces between the other arms (A between C and D, C between B and F, etc.) until all the slack between the arms is taken up and the center is firm. With thread, tie a gold sequin centered with a seed bead over the center of each side of the ornament to hide the wires at the center.

E. CIRCLE with MONOGRAMS, CROSSES, & OTHER SYMBOLS

(Photographs on the front and back covers, this page, page 5, and page 6.)

The dominant feature of this group of Chrismons is the white foam circle. Because it is endless, the circle can symbolize eternity and, by extension, God, the only eternal One. In some instances the circle may also suggest eternal life with God. The circle itself may be decorated with different symbols; various designs may be placed inside it. Among the latter are styrofoam crosses or Chi's and monograms of single or woven lines of gold or pearl beads.

Thus numerous variations—each with its own meaning—of this Chrismon can be made. The picture on this page sets our Lord's cipher in a circle which is adorned with clusters of three beads. It says: The Person Whose birth is celebrated is a Man Whose given name is Jesus. He is a special Man—the Christ—the promised Messiah. More than that, though, the circle declares He is the Son of God and God Himself. He lives eternally in the one God Who shows Himself to mankind in three ways—as the Father, as the Son, and as the Spirit.

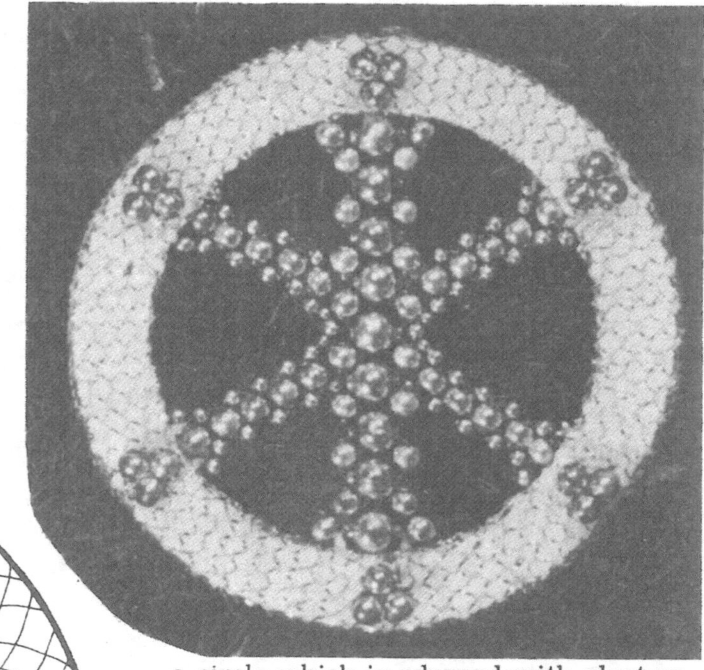

On page 6, another Iota Chi monogram is set in a circle. This time six-point stars decorate the circle to suggest the love of the Father Who gave His only Son to the world.

The design on the front cover combines the sign of the cross with the Chi monogram of the Christ. Christ

FIGURE 7

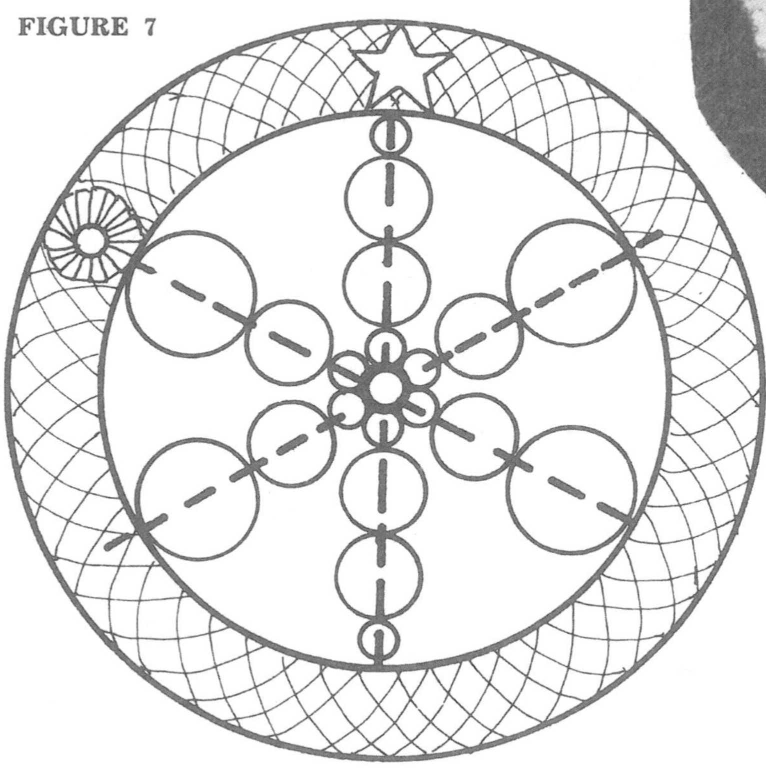

and the cross—can they ever be separated?

The back cover design also combines the cross and the Chi. But the butterfly at the center adds another element to the meaning: By the resurrection (butterfly) of the Christ (X) from the death of the cross (+), all humanity may look to eternal life (o) with Him Whose birth (roses) is celebrated at Christmas time.

If four clusters (earth) of three balls (Trinity) replace the roses as on the colored background pattern on page 25, the meaning of the preceding changes: . . . To eternal life with Him Who lives and reigns with the Father and the Holy Spirit in a world without end.

A variation of this Chrismon is pictured on page 5. The styrofoam cross is used as a Chi which becomes the manger in which the Christ Child lies. A circle of pearls represents the Child. The rose decoration on the manger emphasizes the reference to the Savior's nativity; four groups of roses on the circle underline the fact that, while this was an earthly birth, the Person Who came into the world was also divine.

* * *

Patterns for Chrismon E in half size are Figure 7 on page 24 and Figure 8 on page 25; full size patterns are Figure 9 on page 26 and the colored background of page 25. If the cross or Chi is to be emphasized, use the colored background or Figure 8 pattern on page 25. White styrofoam shows up better against the tree than gold beads. Gold glass rather than metal beads are preferred because only the holes of the former are large enough to carry chenille stems.

The following directions are for any design with a foam cross. After these directions, suggestions for variations are given. The basic "materials" list is the same for all the designs.

Materials: ½" white styrofoam; 6 mm to 16 mm gold glass beads; gold stretch mesh; white chenille stems or pipe cleaners; styro hanger; white glue; fancy gold sequins and/or odds and ends as desired; sequin pins.

Directions:

Cut the circle and cross from one-half inch white styrofoam. If the tools that are used require cutting through the circle, make the cut as shown on double line A on Figure 8. Put styrofoam glue on both cut surfaces; push them together; run a glued three-fourths inch piece of pipe cleaner through the styrofoam as shown at B to keep the circle closed.

Cover the circle with a 2½ inch by 22 inch (2 by 15 inch for the half size) piece of gold stretch mesh. Fit and wrap the mesh so that the raw edges meet on the inside edge of the circle. Anchor it in place with white thread.

Ornament the cross with 5 mm gold sequins-by- the-yard (1/8 inch strips of gold sequin material for the half size) glued to the center front and back of the arms and upright of the cross.

FIGURE 8

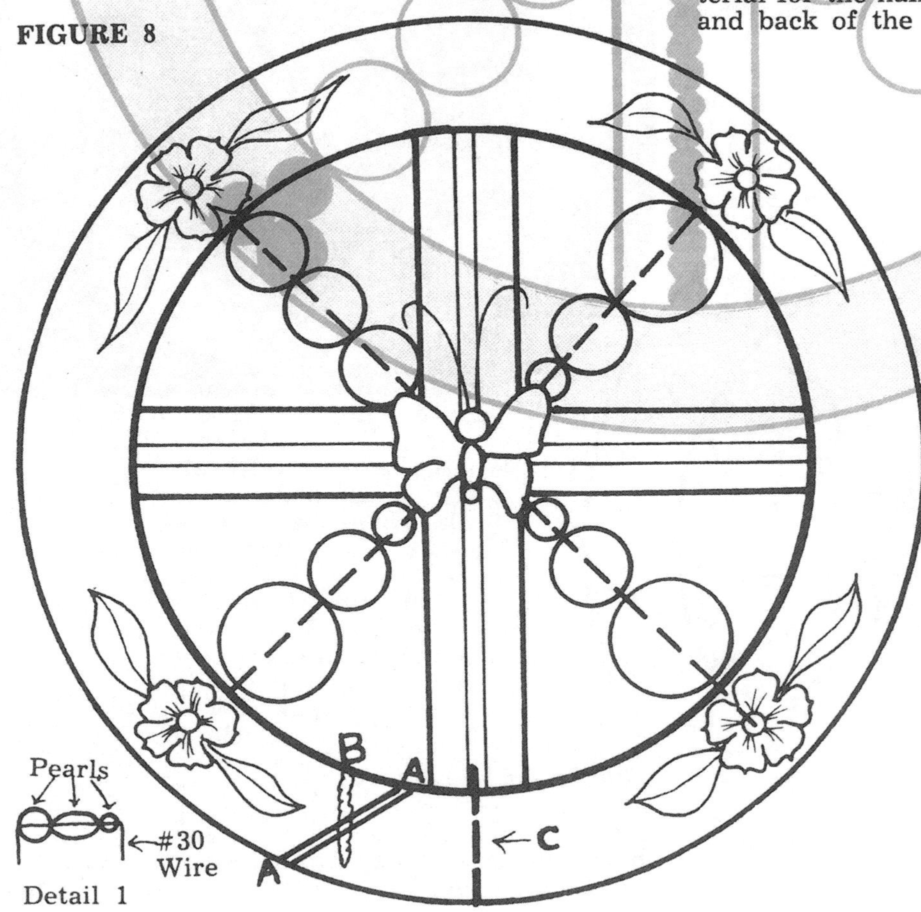

Set the cross in its circle; push one inch pieces of glue-covered pipe cleaners from the outer edge of and through the circle into each cross arm. See C on Figure 8 at the left.

String three 16 mm gold glass beads (or other combination of beads to equal two inches) on each of four three inch pieces of pipe cleaner. (The half size uses a 6, a 10, and a 16 mm or three 10 mm beads on two inch pipe cleaner lengths.) Push one end of a beaded pipe cleaner into the corner of the cross center; curve the cleaner wire so that the other end can be pushed into the foam at the inner edge of the circle as shown. After inserting the four beaded pieces to form the Chi, flatten them. A drop of glue on the ends of the wire holds it in place.

Cut the butterfly from gold foil or paper. Score the rib lines with a stylus

FIGURE 9

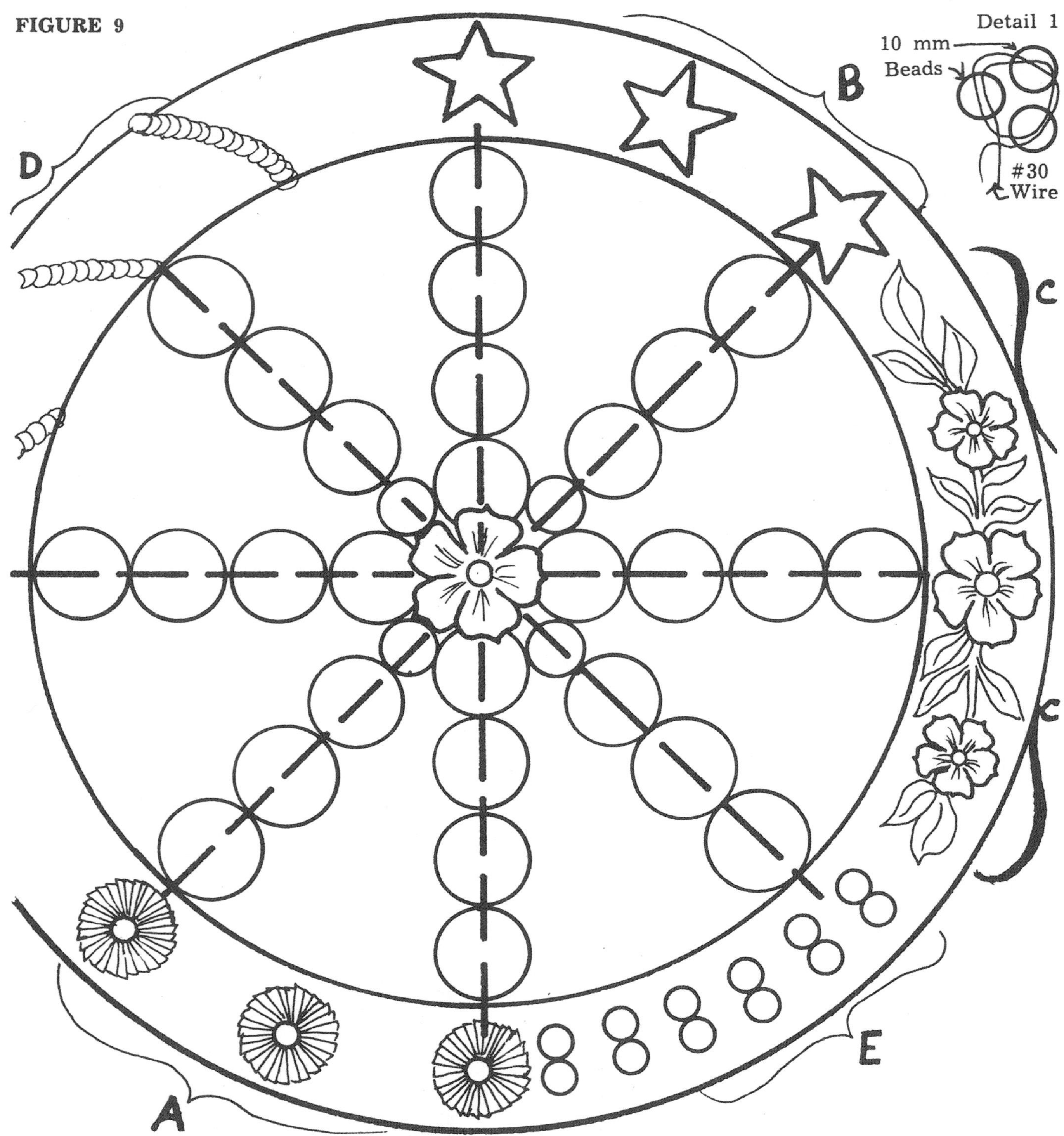

or a ball point pen. Fold the butterfly in the middle so that the wings stand up slightly. Cut two pieces of foil 1/16 by 1 3/4 inches for the antennae. With glue and pins attach the head ends of the antennae and the center of the butterfly to the middle of the cross. Make the head and body of the butterfly of pearls on two pieces of #30 wire (handle as one piece). See Detail 1 on Figure 8. Glue the wire ends; push them into the styrofoam over the wings so that the pearls form the butterfly's body and head.

Circle two pieces of #30 wire (handle as one) through three 10 mm gold beads so that the beads are together and the wire ends extend half an inch as shown on Detail 1 of Figure 9. Glue the wire ends into the circle at the ends of the Chi. Attach a styro hanger at the top of the circle.

* * *

Variations:

If single lines of beads form all the monograms in the circle as shown on Figure 9, string 10 mm and 16 mm beads on chenille stems as shown. No beads are at the center crossover. Insert the ends of the stems into the inner circle edge. Center a 5 mm pearl on a piece of #30 wire; run both wire ends through a 20 mm fancy gold sequin; spread the wires to anchor the sequin close to the pearl. With the leftover wire, attach the sequin to hide the chenille stems at the center and fasten them to hold together. (The half size design on Figure 7 uses 6, 10, and 16 mm beads and a 10 mm sequin at the center.)

The photograph on page 24 shows a woven bead center similar to the weave of the Latin Cross on page 34. The Iota is 10 and 16 mm beads on #30 wire; the Chi uses 6 and 10 mm beads. Bend two-inch pieces of pipe cleaners to a U shape over the #30 wire between beads at the ends of the weave; glue the cleaner wire ends into the inner edge of the foam circle.

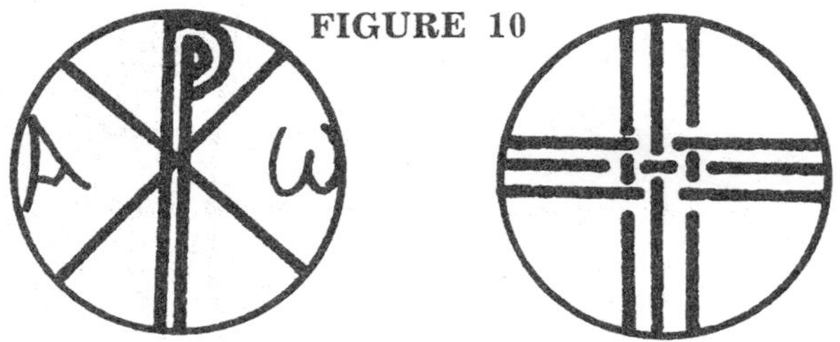
FIGURE 10

Figure 10 at the left diagrams the chenille stems of two more variations of this design. The Chi on the left is made of 10 or 12 mm beads; the Rho is two rows of 6 mm beads. Several pieces of #30 wire are looped in a figure 8 around the stems to hold them together. The Alpha and Omega are 6 mm beads on #30 wire.

The Triparted Cross uses solid lines of 6 mm beads on chenille stems which are woven over and under each other as shown on the pattern.

* * *

When the design and ornamentation of this Chrismon is worked out, the story that it tells must be considered first. Do not decorate with the sole purpose of making a pretty ornament. Let each symbol that is used contribute to the overall message of the Chrismon. Even the ornamental sequin at the center of the design of Figure 9 should add to the meaning.

Five ideas for decorating the circle are shown on Figure 9 on page 26: A—14 mm Sunburst sequins; B—14 mm Epiphany Stars; C—Sprays of leaves and two sizes of rose sequins centered with 5 mm half round pearls; D—5 mm sequins-by-the-yard spiraled around the circle (continuity); E—Pairs of 6 mm beads (dual nature). Or create an original design. Use only ONE design on a circle, and know how it fits in with the total meaning of the Chrismon.

F. SUN OF RIGHTEOUSNESS

(Photograph on the front cover.)

"But for you who fear my name the sun of righteousness shall rise, with healing in his wings." Malachi 4:2.

Materials: 3" white styrofoam ball; 2" gold vinyl festooning; heavy gold aluminum foil; 5 mm gold sequins-by-the-yard; pipe cleaners; gold sequin pins; styro hanger; white glue.

Directions:

Tie a piece of thread around the circumference of a three inch white styrofoam ball to divide it in half. From the patterns on Figure 11 on this page or Figure 13 on page 28 select either the XP monogram for Christ or the IHS monogram for Jesus. Center the pattern on one of the halves of the ball; draw the center line of each letter of the monogram on the surface of the ball with a pencil. Cut lengths of 5 mm gold sequins-by-the-yard to fit the letters; place the sequins on the letters so that the thread that joins the sequins is directly over the pattern lines, which follow the center of the letter. Pin and glue the sequins in place. (Gold braid about one-fourth inch wide may be substituted for the sequins.)

Cut a 10½ inch length of vinyl festooning. Crease it along its length where the fringe and solid material join. Pin the solid band around the circumference of the ball so that the band edge is about one-fourth inch from the circle of thread around the ball and on the side opposite the monogram. See Figure 12 below.

* * *

Cut out right angle triangles from heavy gold aluminum foil—cut six triangles with three

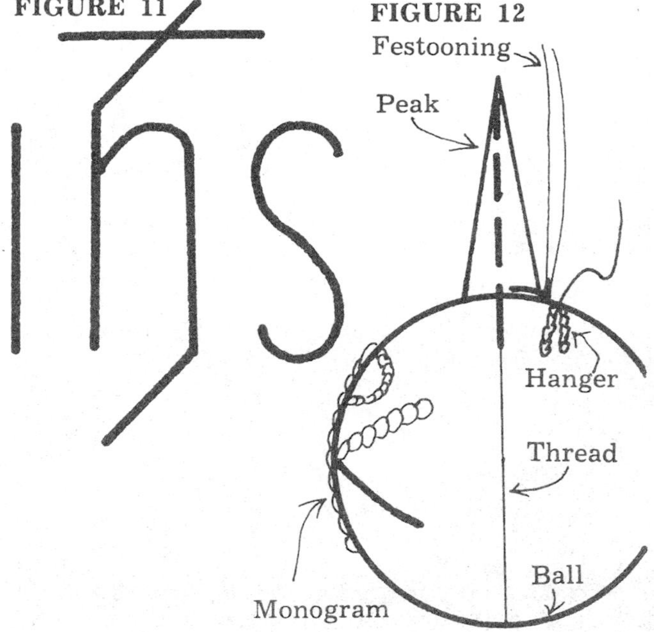

FIGURE 11 FIGURE 12

FIGURE 13

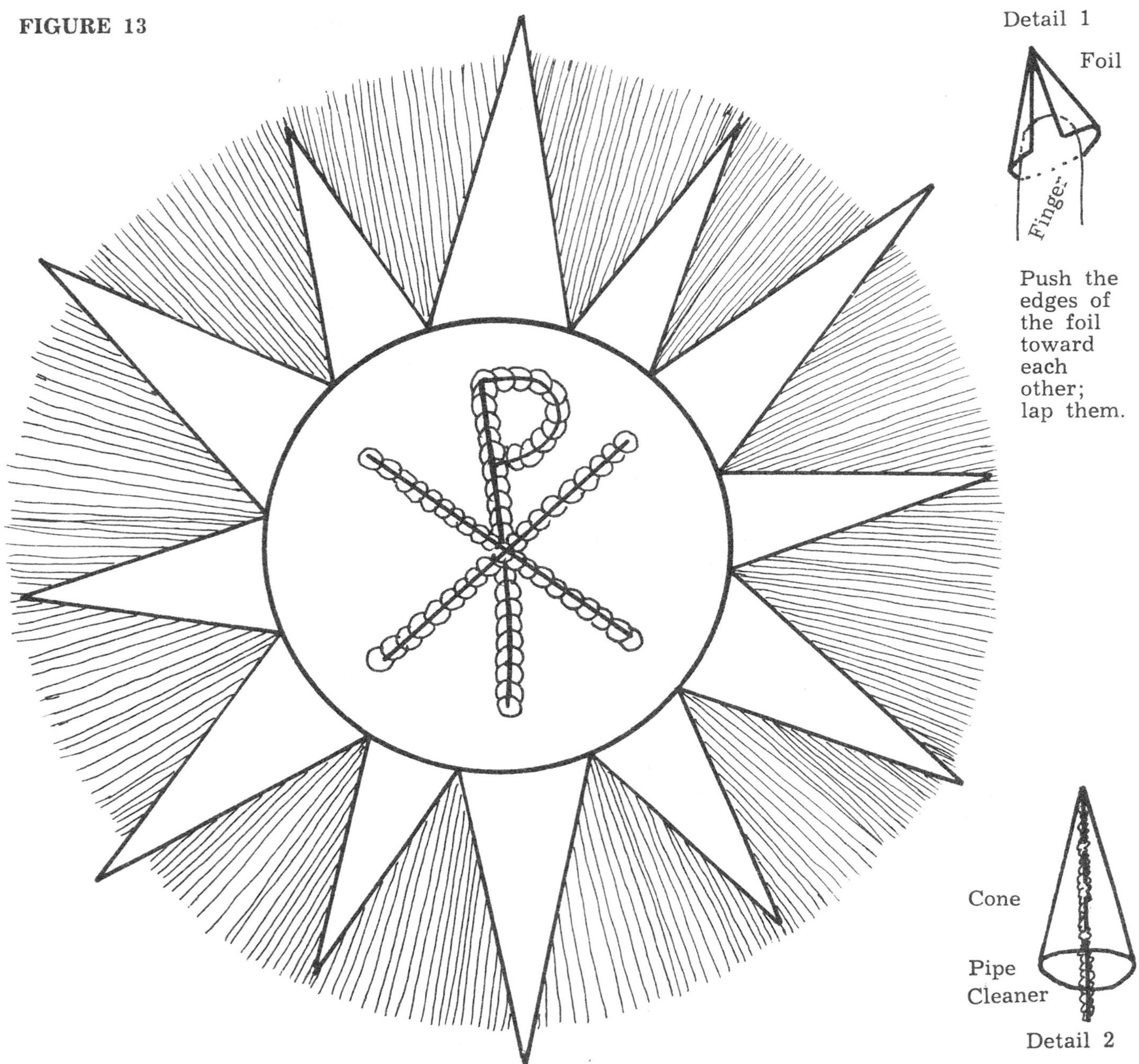

Detail 1

Foil

Fringe

Push the edges of the foil toward each other; lap them.

Cone

Pipe Cleaner

Detail 2

inch legs and six with two and one-half inch legs. Curl the triangles on the finger to form a cone. See Detail 1 of Figure 13 above. The circle at the base of the smaller cones should be about one-half inch in diameter; of the larger cones, about one inch in diameter. Fold the lapped ends of the foil under so that when the cone is set on its base, its peak points straight up. The folds lock the foil into the shape of a cone.

Cut lengths of pipe cleaners—2½ inches long for the larger cones, 2¼ inches for the smaller cones. Put a drop or two of glue inside the peak of a cone; push the pipe cleaner piece into the glue and wedge it into the point. The free end of the pipe cleaner should extend outside the cone at the middle of the base. See Detail 2 on Figure 13 above. Let it dry thoroughly.

* * *

Push the pipe cleaner stems of the peaks into the styrofoam of the ball so that the cones stand out from the ball as shown in the drawings. Alternate the long and short cones. Place the cones in front of the fringe to form a circle around the monogram. Attach a styrofoam hanger at the top of the ball behind the fringe.

* * *

Because this Chrismon is particularly attractive on the tree, it is suggested that several be made. This size is also suitable for home trees. (If the meanings of "circumference," "cone," and the like are not known, consult a dictionary or a teen-age geometry student.)

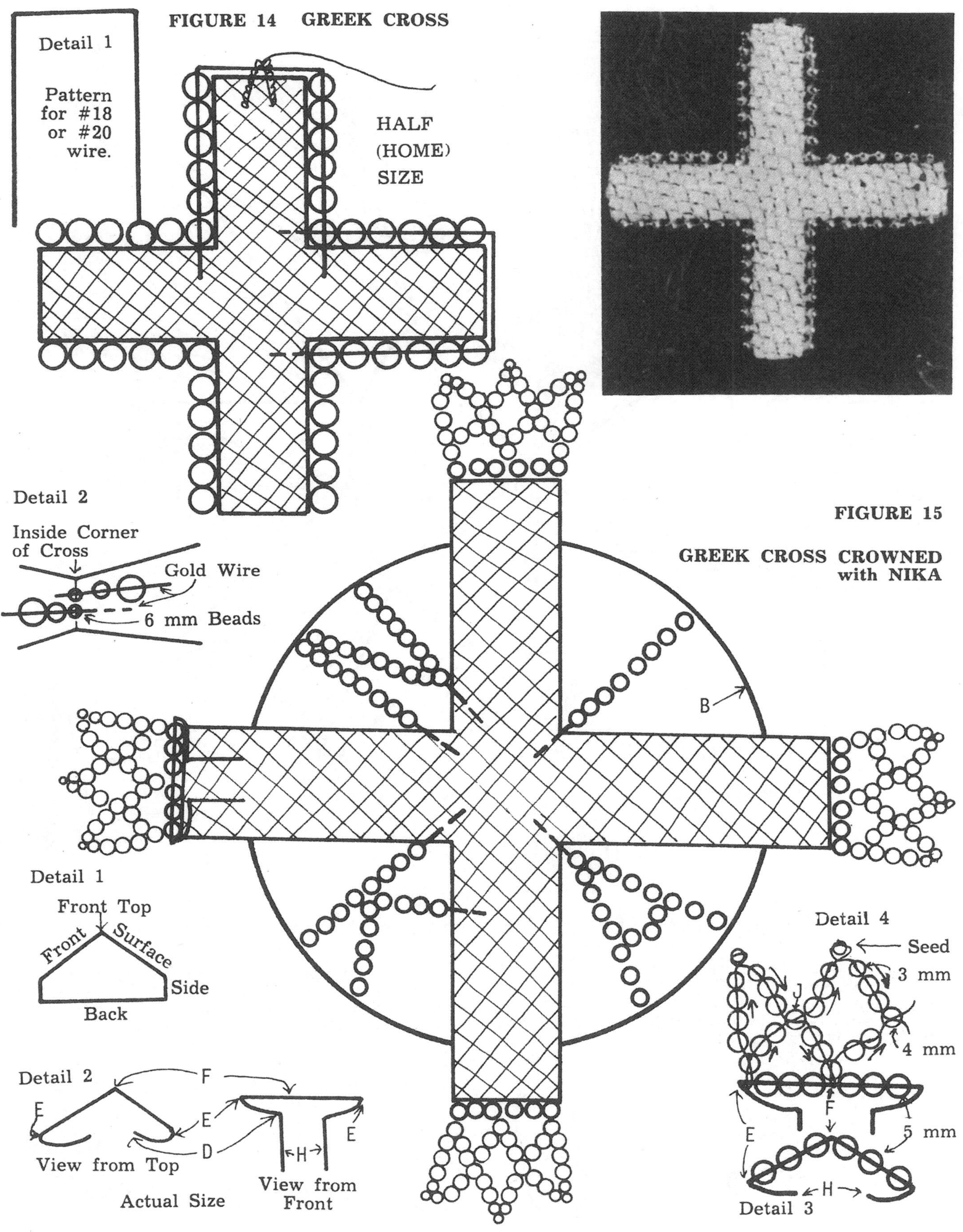
FIGURE 14 GREEK CROSS
Detail 1
Pattern for #18 or #20 wire.
HALF (HOME) SIZE
Detail 2
Inside Corner of Cross
Gold Wire
6 mm Beads
FIGURE 15
GREEK CROSS CROWNED with NIKA
B
Detail 1
Front Top
Front
Surface
Side
Back
Detail 2
F
E
E
D
H
E
View from Top
Actual Size
View from Front
Detail 4
Seed
3 mm
J
4 mm
F
E
5 mm
H
Detail 3

G. GREEK CROSS, CROSS VOIDED, CROSS GAMMADIA

(Photograph on page 29.)

When all extensions of a cross are of equal length, it is called a Greek Cross regardless of the shape of the arms or the designs on their ends. The formal balance of the Greek Cross facilitates its use with other figures (the circle for example) in Christian art.

At one time, use of the Greek Cross showed loyalty to the Eastern Church as opposed to the Western or Roman use of the Latin Cross.

If the beads are the design of this cross, it may be called a Greek Cross Voided or, because it has four Greek Gammas, the Cross Gammadia.

Materials: ½″ white styrofoam; gold stretch mesh; 6 mm gold beads; #18 or #20 gold or copper colored wire; white pipe cleaners; styrofoam hanger; white glue.

Directions:

Cut the cross from one-half inch styrofoam by the colored background pattern on this page for the full size Chrismon or by the half size pattern on Figure 14 on page 29. Cover it with gold stretch mesh; anchor the mesh with thread.

Cut and bend four pieces of #18 gold or copper colored wire to the shape of the pattern on Detail 1 of Figure 14 for the half size or the U shape on the colored background on this page for the full size. (If silver colored wire is used, it must be painted gold before proceeding.)

String eight 6 mm (or six 6 mm for the half size) gold glass beads on each leg of the wire. (If metal beads are used, more beads will probably be needed to equal the length of the side of a cross arm.) Slide a bead strung wire over an arm of the cross toward the adjoining arms, with the beads on each side of the arm. So that one row of beads fits over the other, turn the beaded wire slightly so that the wire on the right enters the arm 3 mm above the middle of the thickness of the arm and, on the left, slightly below the middle. See Detail 2. Push the wires into the cross until the unbeaded wire end is against the end of the cross arm.

Place the styrofoam hanger at the top so that the pipe cleaner straddles the end of the beaded wire to hold the wire in place. Glue U shaped pieces of pipe cleaner over the other three wire ends to hold them against the cross arms.

H. GREEK CROSS CROWNED with NIKA

(Photographs on the back cover and page 6.)

NIKA, the Greek word for conquer, becomes the rays of a rising sun behind this Cross Crowned. This adaptation of the Cross in Glory symbolizes our Lord's glorious victory over sin and death.

Materials: ½″ white styrofoam; gold stretch mesh; 3, 4, and 5 mm gold metal beads; gold seed beads; #20 gold or copper colored wire; #30 wire; clear plastic; foam hanger.

Directions:

Cut the cross from one-half inch styrofoam. Carve the front of the cross to the shape shown on Detail 1 of Figure 15 on page 29. Cover the cross with stretch mesh; anchor it in place.

Cut the circle marked B on Figure 15 from 10 mil clear acetate. Glue it to the center back of the cross; sequin pins through the plastic, glue, and into the back of the arms will hold it.

The letters for *NIKA* may be cut from gold foil or braid and glued to the plastic. Or they may be made of 4 mm gold beads on two strands of #30 wire as shown on the pattern and the back cover. Or weave them of 3 mm and seed beads on beading wire like the picture on page 6. (Adapt the directions from Chrismon FF on page 65.) In the latter two cases, twist the leftover wire from each row of beads into one piece which is one-half inch long. Push these wires through glue into the foam of the cross so that the letter lies as shown on the pattern. Lift the edge of the letter; put a drop of glue under it; then push it back against the clear material to dry.

For the crown, shape #20 wire to the actual size pattern on Detail 2 of Figure 15. The 5 mm beads must be strung on the wire before the shaping is complete; see Detail 3. Notice that line EFE follows the front surface of the cross arm.

Follow Detail 4 to weave the crown. Loop the middle of a piece of #30 wire around the #20 wire at E. Run both wire ends through a 4 mm gold bead. Then run one wire through three 4 mm and a 3 mm bead. Put a seed bead on the wire. Push the beads tight on the wire. Twist the seed bead on the wire to hold its position. On that same wire, string one 3 mm and three 4 mm beads. On the other wire, string two 4 mm beads; run that wire through the last 4 mm bead on the first wire. This is the crossover bead, J. On the lower wire from J, string three 4 mm beads. Loop the wire around the middle of the #20 wire at F. Run the wire back through the bead above F. On the top wire from crossover J, string two 4 mm, one 3 mm, and a seed bead. Twist the seed bead on the wire to hold it in its place. This is half of the crown. Continue to weave beads to the end at E. Back weave to anchor the wires; cut off their excess. Make three more crowns.

Attach a crown to each arm end by pushing the glue-covered H wires of a crown into the end of a cross arm so that the EFE line follows the carved front of the cross arm and the 5 mm beads touch the styrofoam. Attach a styrofoam hanger to the top of the cross behind the crown.

J. LATIN CROSS with ALPHA & OMEGA

(Photograph on the front cover.)

While no one today truly knows the shape of the cross on which our Lord died, the church uses this form, the Latin Cross, most widely. Early Christians often combined the Alpha and Omega with the cross to declare the Savior's divinity. (Any cross which has an upright that extends above the transverse beam and that is tall enough to make the leg longer than any other extension may be called a Latin Cross regardless of the shape of its arms or their decorative ends.)

Materials: #30 gold hair wire; 5 mm & 8 mm pearls; 12 mm or 10 mm & 16 mm gold glass or metal beads. For the half size: 3 mm & 5 mm pearls; 8 mm or 6 mm & 10 mm gold beads.

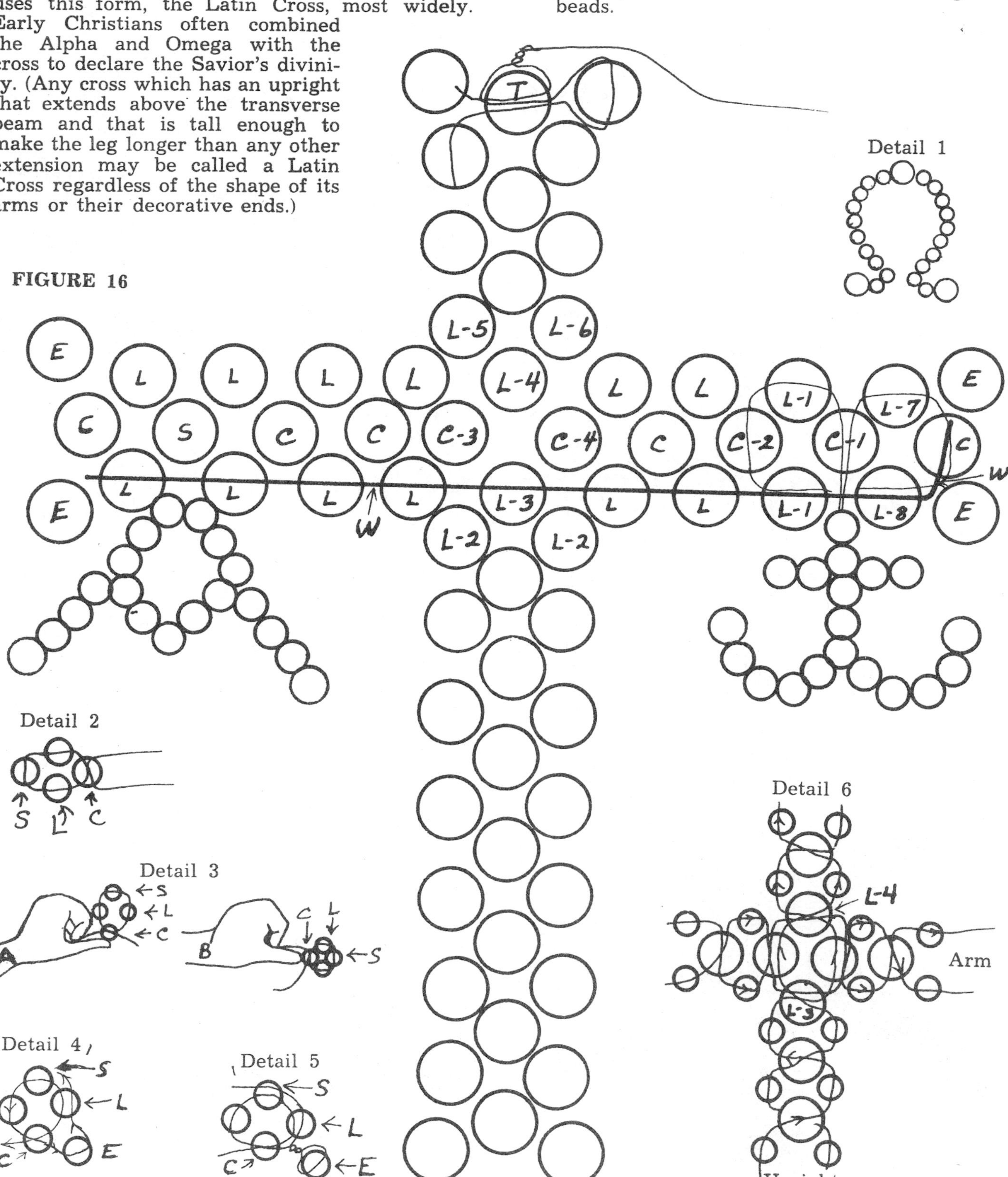

Directions:

Construction of this Chrismon is the same in the full and half size. Directions are written for the full size beads in one size. Make the half size by substituting the smaller beads listed under "Materials." Or use the two bead sizes in "Materials" for either a full or half size cross. In any case, the number of beads and the weaving method is the same.

Figure 16 on page 31 depicts the full size Chrismon in beads of one size. The front cover picture shows this design when it is made of two sizes of beads. The half size cross made by either method is about five inches high.

* * *

First weave the Alpha and Omega of 5 mm and 8 mm pearls by the directions on page 20. Any style of the Omega may be made. Use the number of beads that are on the Figure 16 patterns.

Begin the weave of the arms on the left. Cut a piece of #30 wire three times longer than the finished weave plus six inches. (This is the formula for the amount of wire to use on any "straight" weave except when the finished weave is less than three inches. Then add twelve inches to the triple measurement.) Center four 12 mm gold beads on the 27 inch length of #30 wire. Run one end of the wire through the last bead on the opposite side so that the four beads make a circle. See Detail 2 on Figure 16. Beads S and C are "crossover" beads; wires cross over in them. Beads L are "lengthwise" beads; the wires go straight through them.

* * *

After bead C, hold one wire between the palm and fingers of one hand, the other wire in the same way in the other hand. With the thumbs free, pull the wires tight in a line straight with the bead hole. See A on Detail 3. Without releasing the pull on the wires, push the thumb against C; pull the wires perpendicular to the hole so that they are parallel. (B on Detail 3.) This "anchors" the weave; it makes a sharp bend in the wire next to the bead; it will not slip. The weave must be "anchored" after every crossover bead for the weave to hold its shape.

String another 12 mm bead, E on Detail 4, on one wire. Continue that wire through the adjacent L bead. Pull the wire through L until E is close to, but not against, C and L; the wires that come out of E are of equal length. With one hand, hold the wires where they emerge from the beads; turn E so that the wires from E twist on themselves as shown on Detail 5, the slack in the wires is taken up, and E rests against C. Detail 5 shows the wires loosely strung so that they can be seen; the actual wires must be tight. String the opposite E bead. Then cross over both wires in bead S. Anchor the wires.

String an L bead on each wire; cross over the wires in another C; anchor. Continue the weave of a bead on each wire followed by a crossover bead. This is called a "straight" weave.

After the 10th crossover bead (if the first C and S beads are included), string another E bead on each wire. Cross over the wires in bead C-1; anchor them. Run each wire through its adjacent L-1 bead; cross over in C-2. This process is "back weaving." It anchors the wires before they are cut so that they do not loosen in use. Pull each wire tight; cut each off close to bead C-2. (Diagonal cutting pliers, which can cut close, are the best tool for this job.)

Begin the weave of the cross upright at the bottom in the same way as the arms were begun. After the 7th crossover (count the beads), string two L-2 lengthwise beads. At this point, the weave through the cross arms begins. Beads that were originally lengthwise beads in the arms become crossover beads in the upright. Cross over the upright wires in L-3 of the arm. Run one wire up through bead C-3, the other wire up through C-4. Cross over the wires in L-4. Then string beads L-5 and L-6 on each wire. Continue the weave to crossover T.

When the E beads are put on each side of T, run the wires back through T rather than through an L bead. Carry the wires to the top of T; Twist them together to become the hanger.

* * *

The arms of the full size cross may sag when it is held by the hanger. If glass beads were used, bend #18 stiff green florist wire to line W on the pattern. Work the longer end of the wire through the lower L row from right to left. Then push the 3/8 inch end of the wire up into the right C bead. If metal beads are used, lay the florist wire behind the arm in the groove between the lower L and the C line of beads. Spiral #30 wire around the #18 wire and the weaving wires to hold the #18 wire against the arm.

Attach the Omega to the cross by running the two wires atop the letter up through bead C-1. Run one wire through L-7, down through C, and through L-8. Run the other wire through the top L-1, C-2, and the lower L-1. Cut off the leftover wire. Attach the Alpha to the corresponding beads on the other side of the arm.

Reaching a wire that has been pushed through a bead in a weave is easiest done with needle-nosed pliers. A bead weaver should have a pair.

A kink may develop in a wire when it is run through woven beads. Avoid kinks by keeping the wire straight as it is fed into the bead. Pull the wire through the bead with one hand while the other hand holds the wire taut on the other side of the bead. When the wire going into the bead can no longer be held, put a compass point or a large, strong needle through the loop of wire to hold it taut and keep it from kinking until all of it is pulled through the bead.

Variation, Beads of two sizes:

Detail 6 shows the beading of the crucial point of the cross when it is woven of beads of two sizes. Note that all the crossover beads are the larger size. All the lengthwise beads are the smaller size EXCEPT the two middle arm beads. L-3 and L-4 are the larger size.

K. SERPENT ON THE TAU CROSS

(Picture on the front cover.)

This is a "type" of our Lord's crucifixion, an Old Testament occurrence that parallels an event in Christ Jesus' life. "As Moses lifted up the serpent in the wilderness, so must the Son of man be lifted up."

John 3:14; 12:32 ff; Numbers 21:6 ff.

The fact to remember in this comparison is that the raising of the fiery serpent alone did not save the people. The people lived only when they looked at the bronze serpent on the pole.

Materials: ½" thick white styrofoam; gold stretch mesh; electric wire or cable with a braided jacket insulation, size 12 or 14, from Sear's or an electric supply store; gold paint; 3 mm pearls; #30 wire; white thread; white pipe cleaners. Elective: gold glitter; 5 mm gold sequins-by-the-yard. Half size: substitute ¼" gold cording for the cable, paint, glitter, and sequins.

Directions:

Cut the cross from one-half inch styrofoam by the colored background pattern on this page. The full size cross is cut in two pieces—the upright and the transverse beam. It is joined at the dashed line on the pattern. Cover each section of the cross with gold stretch mesh. Anchor the mesh with white thread. Temporarily join the pieces of the cross by pushing two one and one-half inch pieces of pipe cleaner through the cross bar from the top to the bottom and into the end of the upright.

(The full size cross pattern is outlined in gold. The serpent which is coiled around the cross is in two shades of gold: The solid gold shows the part of the serpent that is in front of the cross; the shaded portions show the parts of the serpent that are back of the cross. The pattern for the half size cross which is cut in one piece from one-half inch foam is solid gold.)

Make the serpent from a 36 inch piece of electric cable. Cut the woven jacket to expose the insulation on one end. Cut out enough insulation to taper the cable to form the tail. Rewrap the jacket around the tail; glue it in place. Or wrap the tail with tape to hold it firmly.

Start at the tail to shape the wire up around the cross to form the serpent. All the shaping must be done with the fingers because the strong cable could break the fragile styrofoam if the cable were bent against the foam. Or the cable may be shaped around a piece of wood cut to the size of the cross upright. The serpent should be curved around the cross, not pressed flat against it. Do not fit it too closely. About one-fourth to one-half inch play for the cross should be left inside the serpent. Cut the cable off at the fang ends. Disconnect the cross bar from the upright. Slide the pieces of the cross out of the cable. From this time on, the shape of the serpent must not be changed.

Cut and shape the end of the cable to form the serpent's head. Strip the two wires inside the cable to make the forked tongue as shown. If glue will not hold the jacket properly around the head, wrap it with tape. Paint the entire serpent gold. Glue 3 mm pearls in place for the eyes. If desired, gold glitter may be applied over the body; also, one row of sequins-by-the-yard may be glued to the length of the serpent from its head to its tail.

Slip the pieces of the cross back inside the serpent. Rejoin the cross at the top, this time with glue on the pipe cleaners and the cross edges that butt. Twist #30 wire around the top loop of the serpent for the hanger.

Half Size:

Since the one-fourth inch cording that forms the serpent in this size is relatively flexible and already gold, the half size construction is easier than the full size. After cutting the cross in one piece, cover it with stretch mesh; anchor the mesh with white thread. Shape the tail; glue it to hold. Wrap, pin, and glue the cord serpent around the cross. Finish the head. A bent #30 wire makes a forked tongue. Insert a styrofoam hanger into the top of the cross.

* * *

Some women object to making this design. If a person to undertake it cannot be found, turn it over to a teen-age boy. He will like the job, and he will do it well. The best serpent that we have ever seen was made by a 14 year old boy.

L. IOTA ETA SIGMA (IHC) IN A CIRCLE

(Photograph on page 34.)

The first three letters of JESus in Greek (or the first two and the last, JEsuS) compose this familiar monogram. The Sigma may be written as S, C, or Σ. The Greek long E, Eta, looks like the Latin n with a tail, η. In Greek, a bar over letters denotes an abbreviation.

When early Greek Christians worked out variations of this monogram of our Lord's given name, some of them extended the upright of the Eta to the abbreviation bar to make a cross. Often this cross-topped Eta looked like a Latin h.

During the dark ages, after the separation of the Eastern and Western Churches, the Romans forgot that this sign was of Greek letters and lost its original meaning. To fill the gap, interpretations based on words in various languages developed. The Latin phrases became most widely known: *Iesus Hominum Salvator* (Jesus, Savior of Mankind) and *In Hoc Signo* (In This Sign.) Phrases in English, German, and other languages can also be quoted.

Because the way that an individual sees a symbol is a matter of personality, such interpretations cannot be called wrong. But they are not historically accurate, and they do not coincide with the originator's intent. The circle around the monogram may suggest eternity and divinity.

Materials: Clear 10 mil acetate; 8 & 16 mm gold glass beads; ½" white styrofoam; white iris glitter; #18 or #20 gold or copper colored wire; #30 wire; gold thread; sequin pins; styrofoam glue.

Directions:

Make a little loop in the end of a 22 inch piece of #18 gold or copper colored wire. Shape the wire to the circumference of a six inch diameter circle. String gold glass or metal beads on the wire. The pattern shows a succession of two 8 mm glass beads followed by a 16 mm glass bead. If desired, other combinations of beads in different sizes may be worked out. After the circle is beaded, make another little loop in the wire to match the first. Cut off the excess wire. Twist #30 wire around the two loops to hold them together and to make a hanger.

Cut a six inch diameter circle from clear plastic. Position the bead circle on the edge of the plastic circle. With gold thread, sew the plastic to the beaded circle by overcasting the thread around the circle wire between each bead and then through the plastic about one-fourth inch from the edge of the circle.

Cut the letters from one-half inch styrofoam by the colored background pattern on this page. (Use either the C or S form.) Carve off the corners of the edges of the front face of the letters so that they peak in the middle. Peaks at the wider parts of the letters will be taller than those on the narrow sections. The colored background of three peaks at the upper left shows the cross sections of wide, medium, and narrow peaked letter parts. Cover the tops and sides of the letters with white iris glitter. Leave the backs of the letters plain.

Position the letters, as shown on the background pattern, on the same side of the plastic as the bead circle is placed. Glue the letters in place. If sequin pins are run through the plastic into the backs of the letters while the glue is still wet, the attachment of the letters will be more durable.

(The letters of this Chrismon may be beaded like those of Chrismon M. Attach them to the plastic with V shaped pieces of #30 wire. Lay the V over wires between the letters, run the wire ends through holes in the plastic, and twist the ends together behind the plastic.)

M. IOTA ETA SIGMA (IHS) ON A GREEK CROSS

(Photographs: Full size on this page; half size on the back cover.)

This design employs the same Iota Eta Sigma monogram that is used on Chrismon L. Its use here on a Greek Cross suggests the sacrifice that our Savior made for our salvation.

Materials: 5 & 6 mm pearls; 6 & 10 mm gold glass or metal beads; #30 wire; #18 green florist wire. Home Size: 3 & 5 mm pearls; 8 mm gold glass beads; #30 wire; pipe cleaners; 5 mm gold sequins.

Directions:

Figure 17 on page 35 diagrams each bead in the letters that make up this monogram. (Lines around the letters separate the cross and the letter beads.) Detail 1 illustrates the beads and weaving method of one-half of a C shaped Sigma if that variation is wanted.

FIGURE 17

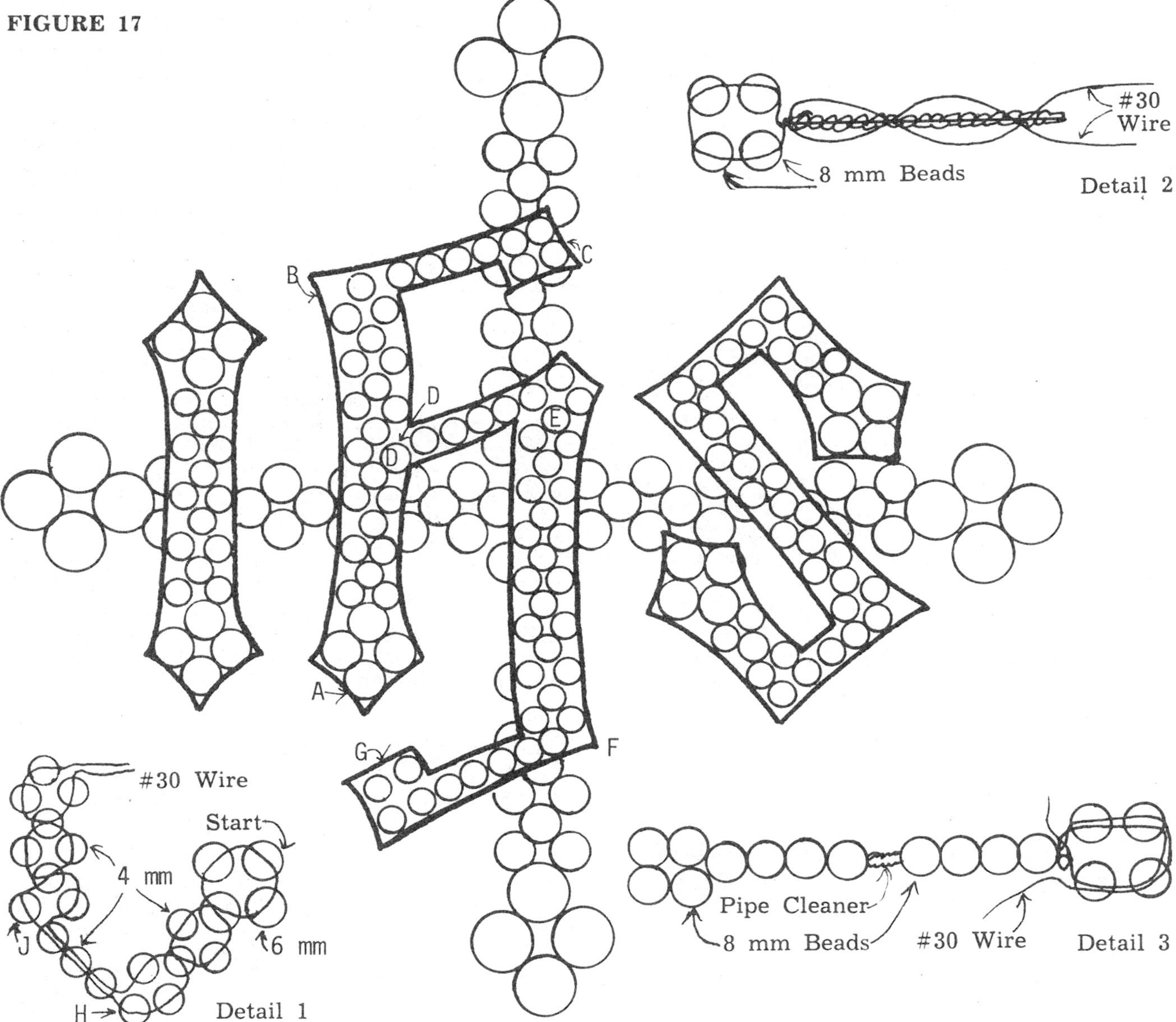

Begin the Iota with a loop of four 6 mm pearls on #30 wire. Cross over the wires in the last 6 mm bead. Continue a straight weave of 5 mm pearls on the lengthwise and crossover beads until four 5 mm crossovers are in the weave. After a 5 mm lengthwise pearl on each wire, end the letter with a loop of four 6 mm pearls. Backweave to anchor; cut off the excess wire.

Weave the Eta (like the Iota) from A toward B on the pattern. After the 8th crossover in the weave when the first bead is included, string two 5 mm pearls on the left wire and one on the right. (This is a corner like H on Detail 1.) String eight 5 mm pearls on both wires. Bend the wires between the 6th and 7th beads to form corner C. Again run the wires through the 5th and 6th beads in the same direction that they first went through these beads. Pull the wires tight; cut one off. Continue the other wire through the 7th and 8th pearls; cut it off.

Run a piece of #30 wire through bead D, which is woven into the AB section. Put the ends of the wire together. String five 5 mm pearls over both wires; push the beads against D; anchor the wires. String two 5 mm pearls on one wire; Cross over the wires in another 5 mm bead, E. Continue the straight weave to corner F, a duplicate of B. Bead the wires from F to G to correspond to BC. Cut off the leftover wires at G.

Follow the pattern to weave either a "C" or "S" Sigma. All the corners of the S type are like corners B. Notice, however, that the beads at the two J corners of the C are different.

* * *

The weave of the cross is like that of the Iota except for the size and number of beads. Each end loop of a cross arm has four 10 mm gold glass beads; the other beads are 6 mm. Twelve 6 mm crossover beads are in the cross arms. After the 6th pair of 6 mm lengthwise beads in the upright, weave through the middle loop of the arm beam. The cross is woven on #30 wire. Leftover weaving wires become the hanger atop the upright. (Further explanations of these weaving terms are under Chrismon J on page 31.)

Arrange the woven letters on the cross as shown. Twist #30 wire around the weaving wires of the letters and cross where they coincide to hold the letters in place. If the arms of the cross need strengthening to support the letters, insert #18 green florist wire through the glass beads or put it behind the metal beads.

The styrofoam letters of Chrismon L may substitute for the beaded letters. Attach them with U shaped pipe cleaner pieces pushed from the back to straddle wires of the cross and to go into the letters in front of the cross.

Home Size:

Weave the letters, by the full size directions, of 3 and 5 mm pearls.

Construct the cross of 8 mm gold glass beads; metal beads cannot be used. Make a loop of four 8 mm beads in the middle of a 16 inch length of #30 wire. Twist the wires tightly to hold the beads in place. Wrap the #30 wires tightly around a 3 inch pipe cleaner piece so that the bead loop is attached at one end of the cleaner and the #30 wires lie smoothly against the pipe cleaner. See Detail 2 on Figure 17. String eight 8 mm beads over the pipe cleaner and #30 wires. String four 8 mm beads on one of the #30 wires; cross over the other #30 wire in these same four beads so that the beads make a loop. See Detail 3. Twist the #30 wires around the end of the pipe cleaner; cut off the excess wire.

Begin the upright in the same way as the arms, but wrap the #30 wires only to the middle of the pipe cleaner; run four 8 mm beads on the wires. Place the upright over the cross arms; twist the #30 wires around the crucial point to hold the arms and upright together. Then wrap the #30 wires around the top of the upright; bead it to the end. Instead of wrapping the ends of the #30 wires around the pipe cleaner to anchor them, twist them on themselves atop the four bead loop to become the hanger.

Position the letters on the cross; wire them in place. Glue a 5 mm sequin at the crucial point of the cross to hide the pipe cleaners.

N. SHEPHERD'S CROOK with ALPHA & OMEGA

FIGURE 18

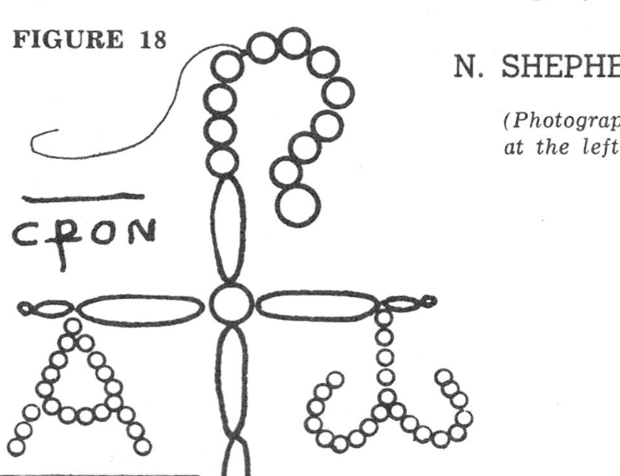

(*Photograph at the left.*)

Several symbols for our Lord are in this simple design. The Alpha and Omega on the shepherd's crook show that this staff refers to the eternal One, the Good Shepherd. The XP and the cross are also apparent.

This basic design was found in the oldest manuscript of Luke, Papyrus 75. When the scribe wrote the Greek word for cross, *stauron,* he abbreviated it by dropping the au and superimposing the T on the R as shown at the upper left of Figure 18. Thus the word contains a figure that looks like a person on a cross.

Materials: 2 or 3 mm pearls; 4, 5, and 3 x 6 mm gold metal beads; gold seed beads; 4 x 20 mm gold beads; 5 mm gold cup sequins; #30 wire. (Five 4 mm or four 3 x 6 mm beads can substitute for each 4 x 20 mm bead.)

Directions:

String a gold seed bead on a 28 inch piece of #30 wire. Put the wire ends together; string a 3 x 6 mm and five 4 x 20 mm gold beads over both wires; push these beads against the seed bead; anchor the wires. On one wire, string the cross arm of a 4 x 20 mm, a 3 x 6 mm ,and a seed bead. Run the wire back through the 3 x 6 mm and the 4 x 20 mm beads to the center of the cross. Hold the cross upright and the wire in one hand; with the other hand, turn the seed bead on the arm to anchor it. Make the other cross arm on the other wire. Twist the two wires around the crucial point of the cross to anchor them.

String one 4 x 20 mm and four 4 mm gold beads on both wires. Pull one wire aside; anchor it. This wire is the hanger. On the other wire, string seven 4 mm and one 5 mm gold bead. Run the wire back through the seven 4 mm beads. Hold the beads and wire with one hand while the other hand turns the 5 mm bead to anchor it. Cut off the excess of the last wire. Shape the 4 mm beads to the pattern to form the crook. Glue 5 mm sequins to cover the wires at the crucial point of the cross.

Make the Alpha and Omega of 2 or 3 mm pearls on #30 or beading wire by the directions on page 20. Attach them to the cross by twisting the wire atop the letters around the cross arm wire.

P. EIGHT-POINTED STAR

(Photographs: Full size on page 38; half size on the back cover.)

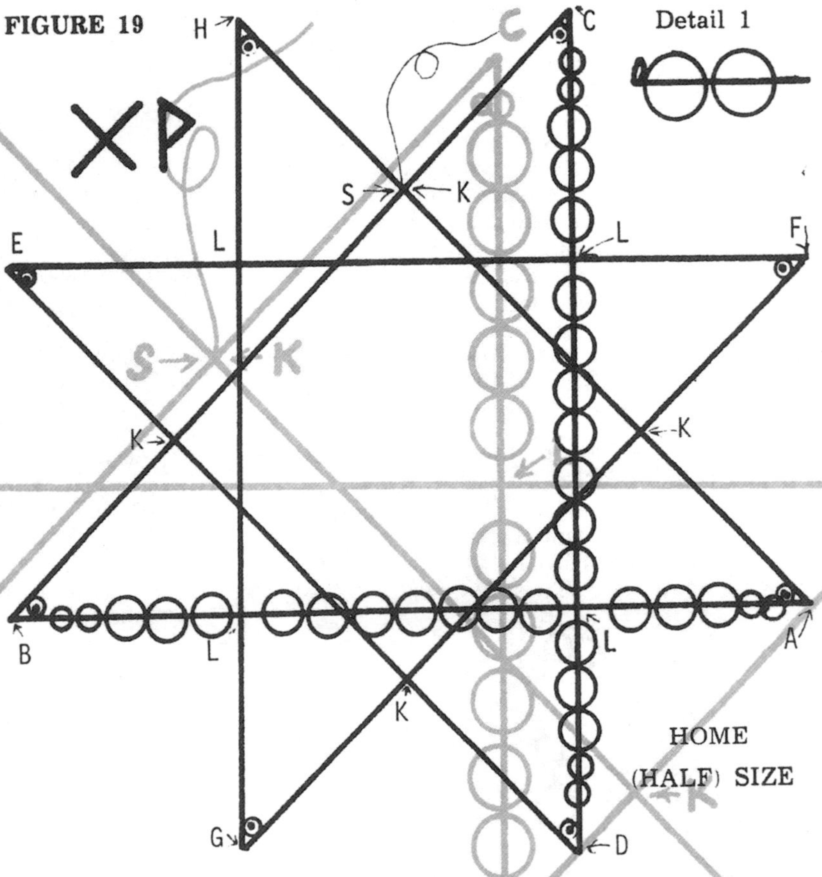

This pre-Christian figure, an eight-pointed star drawn without lifting the tool from the surface, was adopted by Christians as a "concealed" Chrismon during the Roman persecutions. The crossing lines reveal Chi's, Rho's, and crosses to the initiate. When this design is used, one remembers that it was not always easy to be a Christian, not even in name alone.

In Christian symbolism, the eight-pointed star refers to regeneration through Holy Baptism.

I Peter 3:20, 21.

Materials: #18 or #20 gold or copper colored wire; #30 wire; 10 mm gold glass & 4 mm gold metal beads. Half size: 3 & 4 mm gold metal & 6 mm gold glass beads.

Directions:

A person experienced in bending #18 or #20 beaded wires can make this Chrismon with a pair of needle-nosed pliers and the hands. Those without such experience, however, will find it easier to make this design on the jig that is described below.

The colored background pattern on this page is the full size pattern for this Chrismon and its jig; the drawing on Figure 19 on this page is the half size pattern. To make the jig, trace the pattern on paper. Place the paper pattern on a three-fourths inch thick piece of wood. Drive a two inch finishing nail through the circled dot at each pattern point; the nail must be firmly in the wood so that it stands straight. When making this Chrismon, follow the pattern exactly. A mistake in the beginning multiplies as the work progresses.

* * *

With needle-nosed pliers, bend a small loop at the end of a 68 inch length of #18 or #20 wire. (See Detail 1 on Figure 19.) Place the loop at point S on the pattern. Smooth and straighten the wire to lie flat along the pattern line from S to peak A. String thirteen 10 mm gold beads on the wire followed by one 4 mm gold bead. Lay the beaded wire over the pattern; bend the wire sharply around the nail at A. Flatten the wire along the line to B. String one 4 mm, eighteen 10 mm, and one 4 mm bead on the wire. Bend the wire at point B; straighten and smooth the wire to point C.

Continue to string beads and to bend and straighten the wire until it is at point H. In this process remember:

1) The bends in the wires around the nails should be as sharp as they can be made so that the peaks are sharp and the beads cannot run off the wire sections on which they belong;

2) The beads will be loose on the wires to allow for later joining of the design at the K and L points.

When the bending of the wire causes it to lie over the shaped star (the CD line), bend the line of wire over the star and bead that section. Then, take the whole design off the jig, turn it upside down, and put it back on the jig. Make the next bend; straighten the wire; and bead the next section of the wire. Again reverse the design on the jig. Continue this procedure to the end of the design. When the star is complete, a perfect square will be on both the front and back of the design. On one side the corners of the square will be at the K points; the L's will mark the corners of the square on the other side.

* * *

After the H bend, straighten the wire to point S plus one-half inch. Cut off the excess wire. String one 4 mm and five 10 mm beads on the wire. Bend the last half inch of the wire into a loop to match the loop at the beginning. Twist an 18 inch length of #30 wire around the two loops to hold them to each other and to the CB wire. The leftover wire is the hanger.

Twist a piece of #30 wire around the two #20 wires at each K and L point to hold the wires and star firmly together.

* * *

Metal beads may be used instead of the glass beads. When the star is entirely of metal beads however, the beaded wire lines between the points must be shortened.

Half Size:

The half size uses 6 mm glass and 3 mm and 4 mm metal beads. From bend to bend, each line of the star includes a 3 mm gold metal bead, a 4 mm gold metal bead, thirteen 6 mm gold glass beads, a 4 mm metal bead, and a 3 mm metal bead. Count the beads on the pattern to ascertain the spacing between the K and L points.

Q. JERUSALEM CROSS

(Photographs of four variations of this Chrismon are shown. Two are on this page. Another is on page 39 while the fourth is on the back cover.)

A symbol of the crusades, this cross was on the shields of the crusader kings of Jerusalem. Some suggest that the five crosses symbolize the five wounds of our Lord. Another interpretation: The four Tau crosses which make the center cross represent the Old Testament prophecies of a Savior. When the prophecies culminated (were fulfilled) on a hill outside Jerusalem, our salvation was accomplished. The small crosses represent those who take up a cross, follow Him, and proclaim and live the Gospel to the four corners of the world. Thus—the history of Christianity—prophecy, fulfillment, and acceptance throughout the world.

One can use the components of this design as Chrismons. The large cross may be used alone or reduced in size. When the central cross is without the corner crosses, it is called the Cross Potent—a symbol of our Lord's physical and spiritual healing powers. See the Cross Potent on page 58 of *Chrismons for Every Day* for another way to execute this pattern.

Three variations of the Greek Cross hang on the large cross on Figure 20 on page 40. The Southern Cross *(Crux australis)* is taken from nature. It consists of four stars, visible only from the southern hemisphere. The Eye of God *(Ojo de Dios)* is a pre-Columbian art form. Some people see the "eye" as the central symbol of Christianity. The circle around the arms of the Celtic Cross has been variously interpreted as a

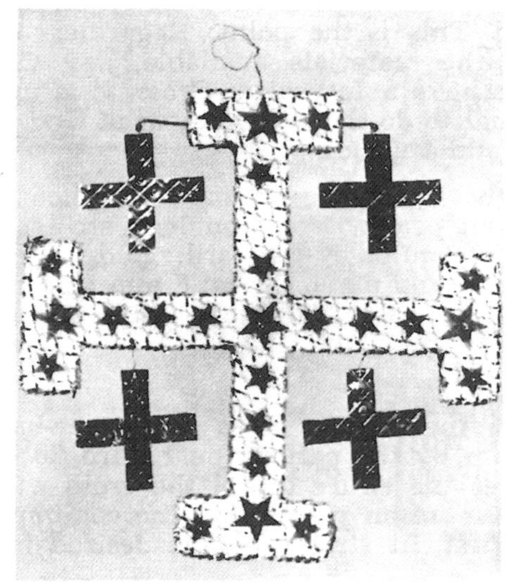

symbol for the sun or eternity. Others believe that the circle was merely a support for the heavy stone arms of the original crosses found in Ireland. Actually no one today knows the actual intent of the device. Another cross which has been interpreted in different ways is the three-barred Russian Cross. Some authorities suggest that the top bar represents the superscription over our Lord's head, the long bar was the arm beam, and the bottom was the foot rest viewed at an angle.

* * *

Several ways of making this design are given as a practical demonstration of how materials and/or construction methods can be substituted in fabricating Chrismons. While the design which is shown on the back cover is difficult and expensive, the one pictured on this page costs only a few cents to make and is within the ability of practically any Chrismon maker. After the materials and directions for the back cover Chrismon are given, ways to vary the construction are outlined. This is the point: Regardless of one's skill or the materials available, any Chrismon tree can have a Jerusalem Cross. It is up to the individual to do the best with what God gives in talents and abilities.

Materials: ½" white styrofoam; either 3, 4, or 5 mm pearls strung on long strings; 5 mm gold sequins-by-the-yard; gold sequin pins; 4 mm gold metal beads; 6 mm gold metal or glass beads; #30 wire; #18 green florist wire; styrofoam glue.

Directions:

Cut the center cross from one-half inch styrofoam by the pattern on Figure 20 on page 40. Cover the entire top of the cross with rows of 3, 4, or 5 mm pearls or some combination of them. First, fit strands of the desired beads on top of the cross to ascertain whether 4, 5, or 6 rows are needed to cover the width of the cross arm. Then glue the first row of pearls around the outer top edge of the cross.

Loosely strung pearls turn the corners most easily. Pressing the pearls slightly into the styrofoam to make indentations in the foam before applying the glue simplifies the work. Put a line of white glue around the edge of the cross where the outer row of pearls is to go. Use no more glue than can be worked before it dries. Set the pearls in their holes on the glue; hold the beads in place with straight pins stuck into the styrofoam on each side of the row. Allow the pins to stay in place until the glue is dry enough to hold the beads but not so dry that the pins stick. After the first row is dry, place the next row around the cross just inside the outer row. Continue gluing pearls in place until the entire top of the cross is covered.

After the glue that holds the pearls is completely dry, pin two rows of 5 mm gold sequins-by-the-yard around the outer edge of the cross to cover the sides of raw styrofoam.

Weave four Greek Crosses on #30 wire by the Detail 1 pattern on Figure 20. Four millimeter metal beads make up the outer (lengthwise) beads while six millimeter beads are the center (crossover) row as well as the four center beads of the cross. (Weaving directions are on page 31.)

Bend one end of a 5 inch length of #18 green florist wire to make a tiny loop. Run the wire through the center of the top Tau cross as shown by the dotted line on the pattern. Make a loop at the other end of the wire. Attach a Greek Cross to each of these loops. Attach the lower crosses by running the leftover wire from their weave up through glue and the arms of the center cross. The lower crosses should be directly under the upper crosses. Place a loop of #30 wire just below the cross bar of the top Tau for a hanger. Twist it behind the cross to hold it in place as invisibly as possible.

Alternate Construction Methods:

The cross pictured on this page is cut from free packing foam and sprinkled with gold glitter. (White iris glitter could be used as well.) The corner crosses are cut from another type of packing foam by the Detail 3 pattern on Figure 20. Styrofoam hangers fasten the corner crosses to the central cross in the same manner as the beaded crosses above were attached.

The cross shown at the right on page 38 is cut from one-half inch white styrofoam. Cover it with gold stretch mesh; anchor the mesh in place with thread. Pin and glue 10 mm Epiphany Star sequins around the edge of the center cross. Cut the small crosses from gold foil, sequin material, or two pieces of gold backed paper glued together. Use either the Detail 2 or the Detail 3 pattern. With a stylus, score the foil along the lines. Then turn the foil over and score the circles on the other side. Punch a hole at

FIGURE 20

Detail 1
Detail 2
Pin along edge to hold pearls.
S
Detail 3
Detail 4
Southern Cross
Detail 5
Eye of God
Detail 6
Eastern (Russian) Cross
Detail 7
Celtic Cross

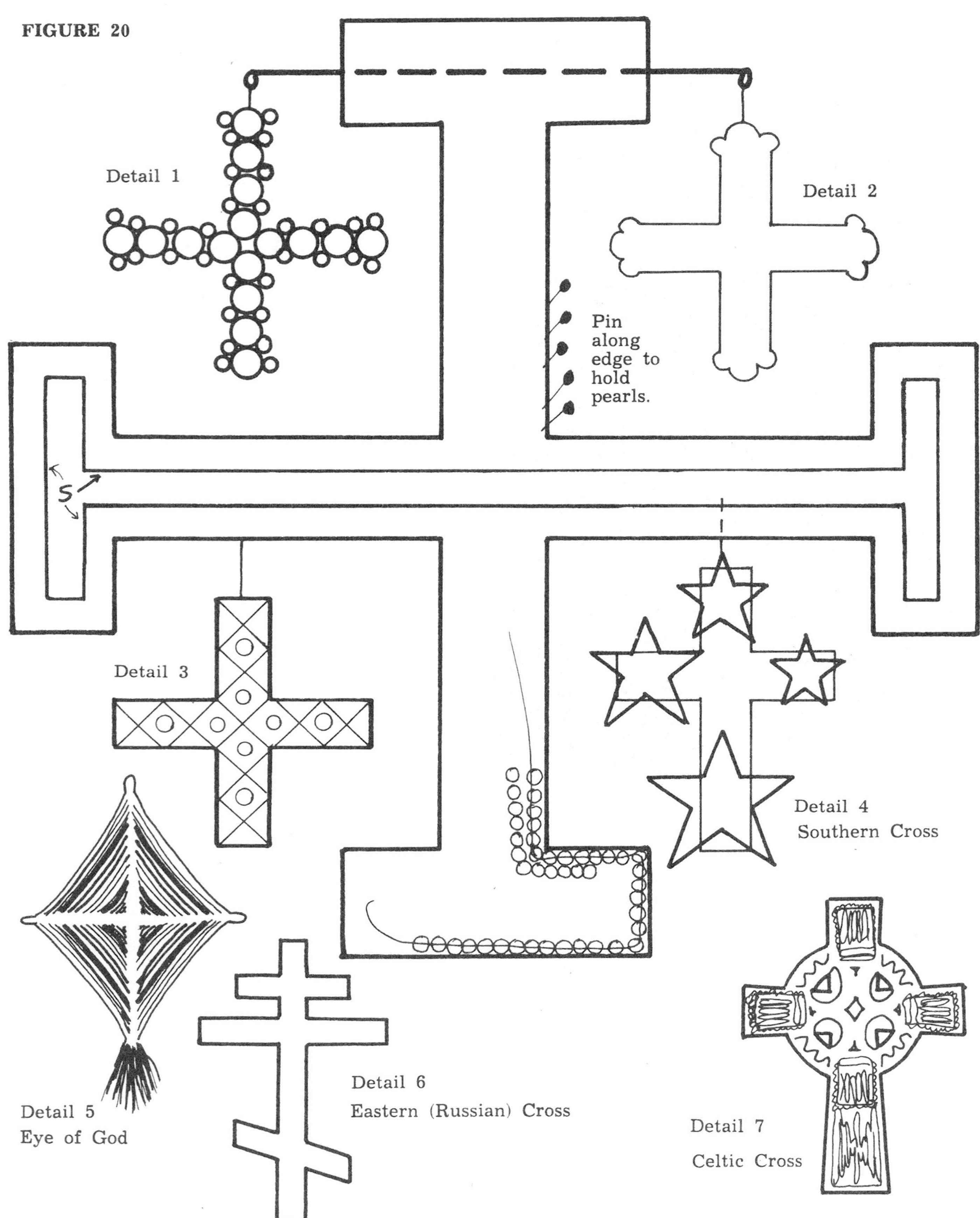

the top of the cross. Run a #30 wire through the hole; twist it to hold. Attach the corner cross to the central cross with this wire. A styrofoam hanger goes atop the main cross.

The cross on the left of page 38 is woven of 8 mm pearls on two strands of #30 wire which are handled as one. After the body of the cross is woven, the T crossbars are added. Bend #18 green florist wire to the shape shown by line S on the horizontal beam pattern. This support is attached to the back of the arms with #30 wire; another like it is fastened to the back of the upright of the cross to hold it rigid. The beaded corner crosses may be used. Or, directions for the Cross in Eternity may be adapted to make Greek Crosses of single rows of 10 mm gold glass beads on pipe cleaner pieces.

* * *

Changes need not be confined to construction procedures. Why not use imagination to tell the story in a new way, to make the message clearer? Is there a better way to say that the Gospel is for all people throughout the world than by using four identical crosses in the corners? Why not make each cross different? Why not let each cross point to a specific compass direction, suggest a particular people or culture?

For the north, use the Celtic Cross made long ago by an ancient people on a northern island. Depict an eastern church with the three-barred Russian Cross with its echo of the Byzantine. Take the Southern Cross from the heavens to represent the people on whom it shines. And use the *Ojo de Dios* from the American Indians of the west.

Cut the Celtic and Russian Crosses and the Eye of God from gold material. Score their designs with a stylus. Or, make the Celtic and Russian Crosses by the directions on page 17 in *Chrismons for Every Day;* ask a friend in the southwest to weave a white and gold "eye" in the needed size. Cut the stars of the Southern Cross from gold foil by the pattern. Glue them to a transparent plastic cross. If others are to recognize the *Crux australis,* the size of each star must follow the pattern. They are drawn in these sizes to show their magnitude.

R. CROSS AND CHI

(Photographs: Half size on the back cover; woven bead cross and Chi of roses on page 6; styrofoam cross and Chi of roses on this page.)

The Greek Chi (X), the first letter of CHrist, combines with the cross. The Christ and the cross—can we ever separate them? Only when we understand both the Christ and the cross can we begin to see the measure of God's love.

* * *

This is another Chrismon which may be made in several ways. Method I, which is illustrated on the colored background of page 42, is the easiest II, III, and IV are progressively more difficult and expensive but also, for some, more attractive. Studying the various methods will give ideas for substitutions when they must be made.

Materials: Supplies depend on the construction method selected; see the directions for each.

METHOD I:

Cut the symbol from one-half inch thick white styrofoam by the full or half size pattern on the colored background on page 42. Cover the cross and Chi, either lightly or heavily, with gold or white iris glitter. Or, give the styrofoam a smooth pearlized finish.

Adorn the center and arm ends of the cross and/or the Chi with white and/or gold sequins to tell the desired story. Sequins from 5 mm to 20 mm size may be used. Let the ornamentation contribute to the Chrismon's message. Glue a styrofoam hanger into the top of the cross.

METHOD II:

(Illustrated on this page.)

Cut the symbol from one-half inch styrofoam by the full or half size pattern on the gold background on page 42. Cover the symbol with gold stretch mesh; anchor it with white thread.

To symbolize the Nativity, cover the entire Chi with white or gold roses about one-half to one inch in diameter. Or, cover the entire cross with white or gold butterflies about three-fourths inch large to suggest the Resurrection. Or, place one large rose or butterfly (about two inches in diameter) at the center. Attach a styrofoam hanger at the top.

FIGURE 21

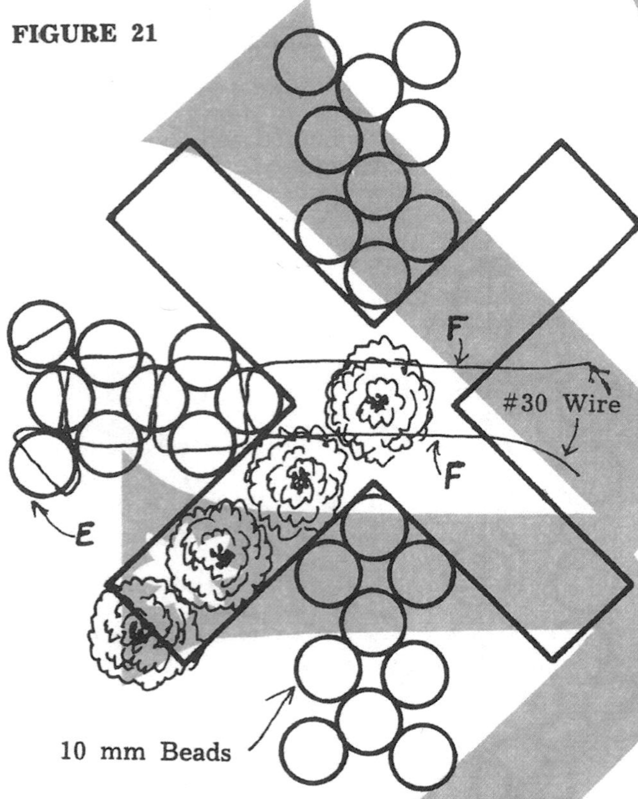

METHOD III, Half Size:

(Illustrated on the back cover.)

Figure 21 on this page above is the half size pattern for this design. Cut the Chi only from one-half inch white styrofoam. Cover the letter with gold stretch mesh; anchor it with thread. (The mesh covered side is the back of this design.)

Weave the cross of 10 mm gold glass beads on #30 wire. Start at the outer end to weave toward the center as shown at E on the pattern. When the beads equal those on the pattern (count them), thread each weaving wire on a long needle. Run the wired needles through the center of the styrofoam Chi as shown at the F's. On the other side of the Chi, take up the wires to weave the opposite arm of the cross to its end. Back-weave to anchor the wires; cut off their excess.

The vertical of the cross is woven from the bottom in the same way except that the ends of the weaving wires become the hanger at the top.

Glue three white roses, each three-fourths inch in diameter, to each arm of the Chi. At the center of the design, place either a gold or a white rose of the same size.

Full Size:

Except for the following changes, the full size design is made in the same way as the home size: Use the gold background pattern on this page for the full size cross. Set three one inch roses on each arm; center the design with a one and one-half inch rose. Weave the cross of 16 mm gold glass beads; make three loops of beads in each arm instead of the two loops on the half size. The cross arms need a #18 green florist wire reinforcement as explained in the general weaving instructions on page 31.

FIGURE 22

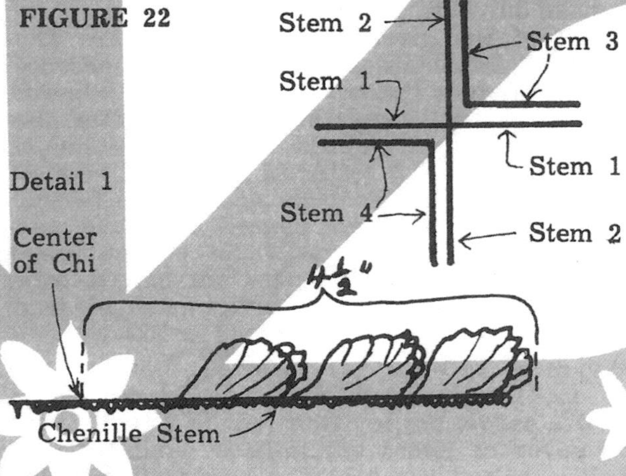

METHOD IV:

(Illustrated on page 6.)

From the directions for Chrismon J on page 31, weave a Greek Cross of 16 mm gold glass beads. Use the same number of beads in both the vertical and horizontal of the cross as are in the arms of Chrismon J. Reinforce the arms with #18 green florist wire.

Lay four seven inch chenille stems together as shown on Figure 22 on this page above. Notice the right angle bends at the middle of two stems. Twist #30 wire around the stems to hold them together in the Chi shape.

Place the middle of the woven bead cross over the center of the Chi. Mark the points on the Chi where it comes out from under the woven beads. From these points outward, arrange three or four white plastic roses (about ¾ to 1½ inches in diameter) on the legs of the Chi so that the end of the last rose on each leg is about 4½ inches from the center of the symbol. See Detail 1 of Figure 22. Spiral #30 wire around the chenille stem and the stems of the roses to hold the latter in place. Spiral two inch gold vinyl festooning around the chenille stem between the roses so that the festooning flares out behind the roses. Begin the spiral at the end of each Chi leg; carry it to the center of the cross. Glue or wire the ends of the festooning to the chenille stem.

Place the Chi under the cross. Wire the two symbols together with #30 wire at the points where they cross over each other. Either a butterfly or another white rose may be wired on top of the center beads.

* * *

To make this design in the half size, use 8 mm gold glass beads and proportionally smaller roses. The chenille stems are only 4½ inches long.

S. IOTA CHI with DAISIES and LILIES-OF-THE-VALLEY

(Photograph on the front cover.)

Iota (I), the first letter of Jesus in Greek, combines with a Chi (X), the first letter of Christ, to make our Lord's cipher, an interwoven abbreviation of His given name and His title. The Iota is made of daisies to point to the innocence of the Child in the manger while the lilies-of-the-valley that form the Chi symbolize the Christ's humility.

FIGURE 23

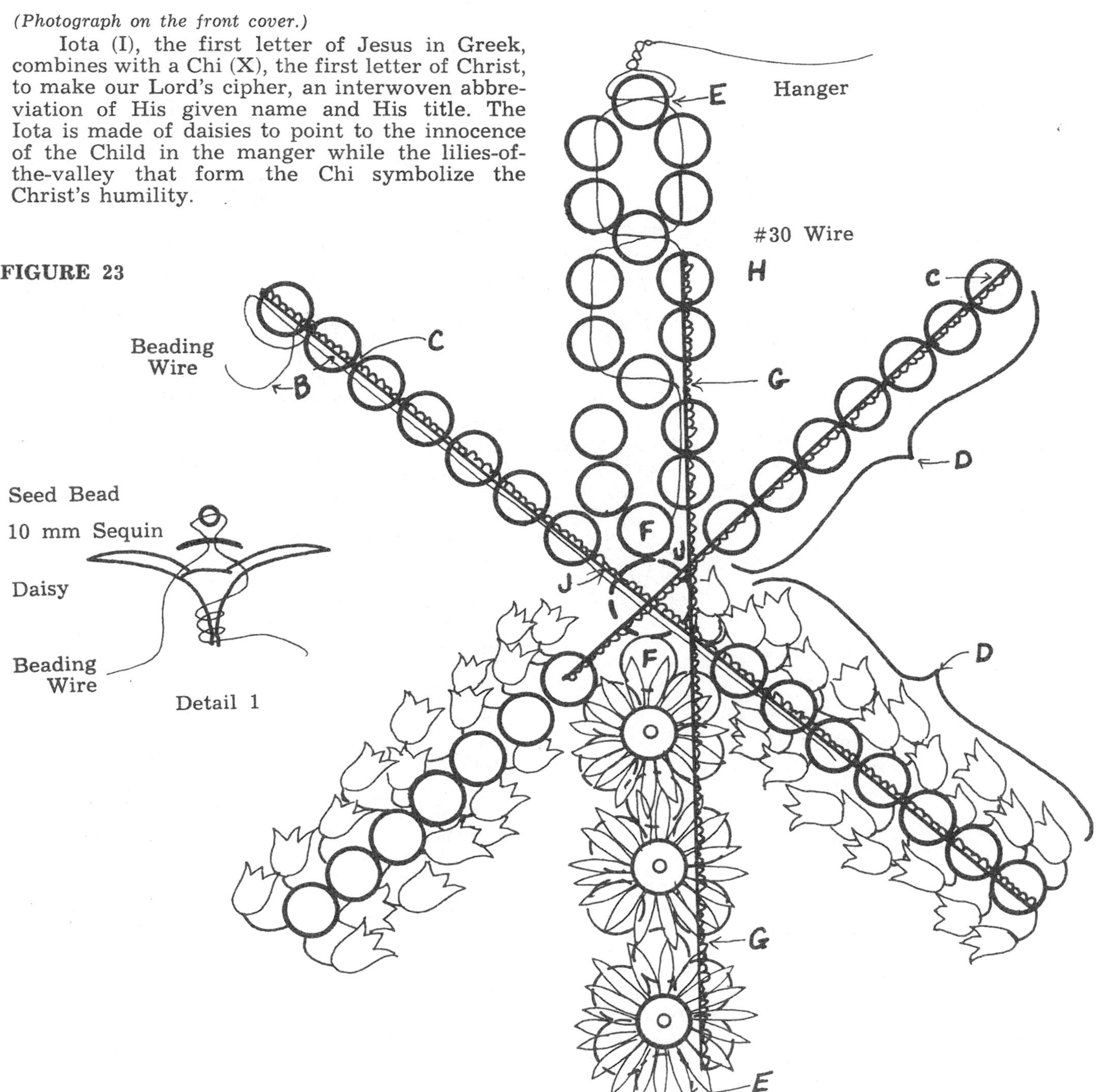

Materials: 10 mm gold glass beads; 10 mm gold cup sequins; gold seed beads; permanent flowers: white lilies-of-the-valley and white daisies; white chenille stems; #30 hair wire; gold beading wire. (If metal beads are used, several construction details must be changed, and #18 green florist wire must be substituted for the chenille stems.)

Directions:

On each of two 6¾ inch lengths of chenille stems, C on Figure 23 on this page above, string fourteen 10 mm gold glass beads. Run a 28 inch length of gold beading wire through the 10 mm beads on the stem and alongside the chenille stem. Arrange the beading wire so that 10½ inches of the excess wire extends on each end of the stem. See B on the diagram. Push seven of the 10 mm beads to each end of the stem. (Note the D sections.) Carry the beading wire around the last bead on each stem end to the stem between the last and the second last bead; twist the beading wire around the chenille stem to hold the outside bead on the stem firmly.

Position two white lily-of-the-valley racemes behind each group of seven beads. Place the stems of the lilies behind the chenille stems so that the lily bells show on each side of the gold beads. Spiral the beading wire (from the end bead toward the center of the X) around the lily stems and the chenille stem to hold them together. At the center of the Chi, use the leftover beading wires to fasten the two chenille stems together where the stems cross over each other to form the X.

Begin to weave the Iota on #30 wire at the bottom E bead. The straight weave of 10 mm gold glass beads has two 10 mm beads on each lengthwise wire as shown on the pattern. After the lower F bead is woven, anchor the wires. Push a 5½ inch chenille stem (G) up through one side of the woven beads to the position where bead H will be. Push another stem up through the other side of the weave. Wrap and twist each #30 wire from the lower F bead around its corresponding chenille stem to the point where the upper F bead is to be woven. Continue the weave of 10 mm beads to the top E bead. As the lengthwise beads are woven on the #30 wire, they are also run over the G chenille stems. The leftover #30 wire at the top becomes the hanger. The total length of the Iota is seven inches. Notice that the stems have no lengthwise beads on them at the center.

Cut off the stems of artificial white daisies to a length of one-fourth inch. Cover the yellow center of each daisy with a 10 mm gold cup sequin attached with beading wire as shown on Detail 1 on Figure 23. After the beading wire is twisted around the stem of the daisy, run the stem and wire through the center of a circle of beads on the Iota. Twist the leftover beading wire around the weaving wires of the Iota to hold the daisy in place. Set a daisy at the center of each loop of beads.

Position the Iota over the Chi. With #30 wire, fasten the chenille stems together at the four J points at the center of the cipher. Attach a 16 mm gold bead at the center to cover the wires and stems. Or, center the design with a white or gold butterfly to emphasize that this is the cipher of the One Who is risen.

T. CHRISTOGRAM with CROSS, CHI RHO, TRIANGLE, & M

(Photograph on the back cover.)

The Chi Rho and the cross are readily apparent in this design. A triangle symbolizes the Holy Trinity and points to our Lord's divine nature while the M, a monogram for His mother, Mary, suggests His humanity. The rose decoration on the design further emphasizes the fact of the Christ's birth as One of us.

The shells which cover the triangle evoke thoughts of another birth—birth in Christ. Shells traditionally symbolize Holy Baptism; they remind us of our second birth, our spiritual rebirth at baptism when, by faith, we become children of God. Galatians 3:23 ff.

Materials: ½" thick white styrofoam; crystal or white iris glitter; assorted 12 to 20 mm gold rose and leaf sequins; 14 mm white iris shell sequins; gold sequin pins; styrofoam hanger.

Directions:

Cut the Chrismon from one-half inch white styrofoam by the colored background pattern on page 45. (This design is the most difficult to carve with a knife in the Basic Series. If a hot wire machine is available, however, it is relatively easy. Other steps in the construction are simple.) After the Christogram is cut out, slice away the styrofoam on the face of the two top sides of the triangle so that they appear to go behind the cross arms as shown on Figure 25.

Glue a styrofoam hanger at the top of the upright of the cross. Cover the back and the sides

FIGURE 24

HALF (HOME) SIZE

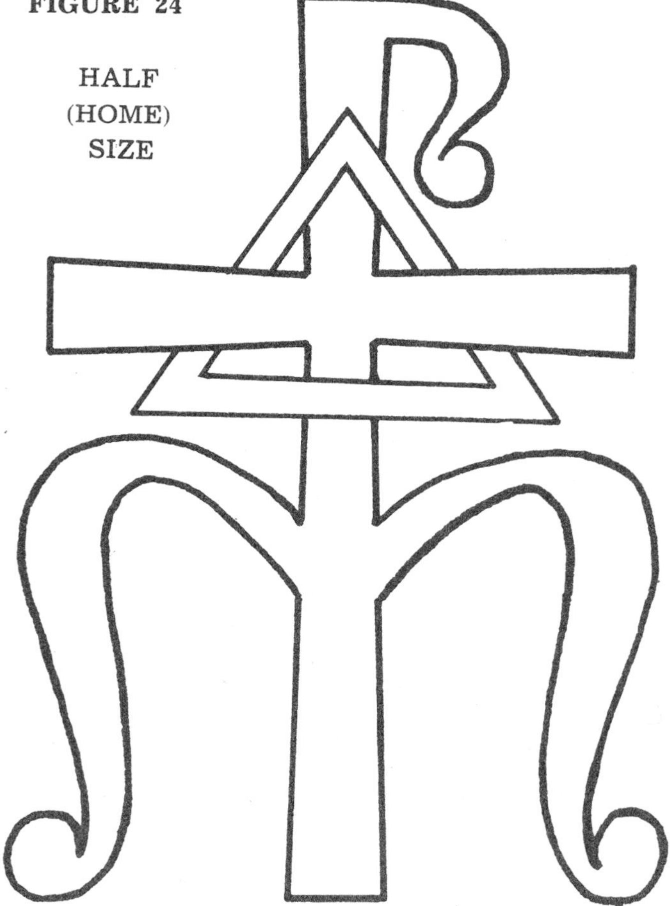

of the design with white, white iris, or crystal glitter. Pin and glue a row of 12 mm white iris shell sequins to cover the triangle except for the parts that go under the arms of the cross. Note that shell sequins can go into the sides of the cross arms to cover the gap that was made in the triangle sides by the hot wire machine when the inside of the triangle is cut out.

Make an arrangement of gold rose and leaf sequins in different sizes to cover the M and the Chi Rho. Use the larger sizes of sequins where the letters are widest; the smaller leaves taper down to the narrower parts. Figure 26 on this page at the right and the picture on the back cover show how the sequins may be arranged. Pin and glue the sequins in place. Glue a 5 mm half-round or a 5 mm round pearl at the center of each rose.

Home Size:

Cut the design from one-half inch thick white styrofoam by the pattern on Figure 24 on page 44. Cover the entire front, back, and sides of the Christogram with white iris or crystal glitter. If they are wanted, very small white shells may be glued to the triangle. Likewise, gold rose and leaf sequins may be attached to the cross, the Rho, and/or the M. Or, only the M may be decorated. Or, the Christogram may be ornamented only with glitter. Glue a styrofoam hanger at the top of the upright of the cross.

If you are near the ocean—or visit there—why not let the youngsters look for real shells, little white ones, to cover the triangle?

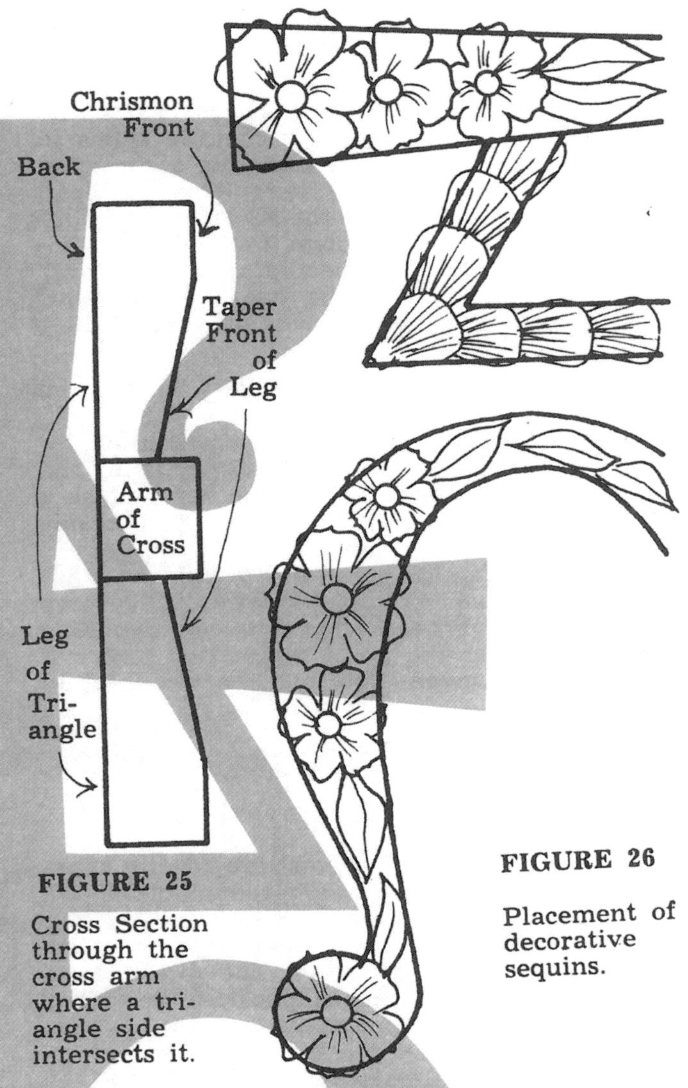

FIGURE 25

Cross Section through the cross arm where a triangle side intersects it.

FIGURE 26

Placement of decorative sequins.

U. TRIQUETRA AND CIRCLE

(Photograph on page 46.)

The Trinity in Eternity!
The Eternal Triune!
The Eternal One!

The endless circle suggests eternity, God—the only eternal One, or eternal life with God. The triquetra, a complete figure which is composed of three separate and equal arcs, symbolizes the one God Who showed Himself to man in three separate and distinct Persons. These ideas may be combined to proclaim a variety of truths.

Materials: 6 and 8 mm pearls; 10 mm gold glass beads; #20 silver colored wire; #18 or #20 gold or copper colored wire; #30 wire.

Directions:

Make a loop, A on Figure 27 on page 46, at the end of a length of #20 silver colored wire. After the loop, bend the wire to the AB semicircle, the first arc of the triquetra. String twenty-four 8 mm pearls on the wire to make the AB arc. With needle-nosed pliers, bend the wire at B. (The one-fourth inch play of beads on the wire allows space for the joining of the arcs after all of them are strung.)

Shape the next arc, BC, of the triquetra by the pattern. Run another 24 pearls on the wire; bend the wire at point C. Make the third arc, CA, in the same way. At the end of the arc, make a loop in the wire to fit over the first loop at A. Cut off the excess wire.

Lap the arcs over and under each other as they are shown on the pattern. With #30 wire, fasten the two end loops together; the leftover wire is the hanger. Wrap #30 wire around the two wires of the triquetra where they cross over each other at the three D points. Count the beads

FIGURE 27

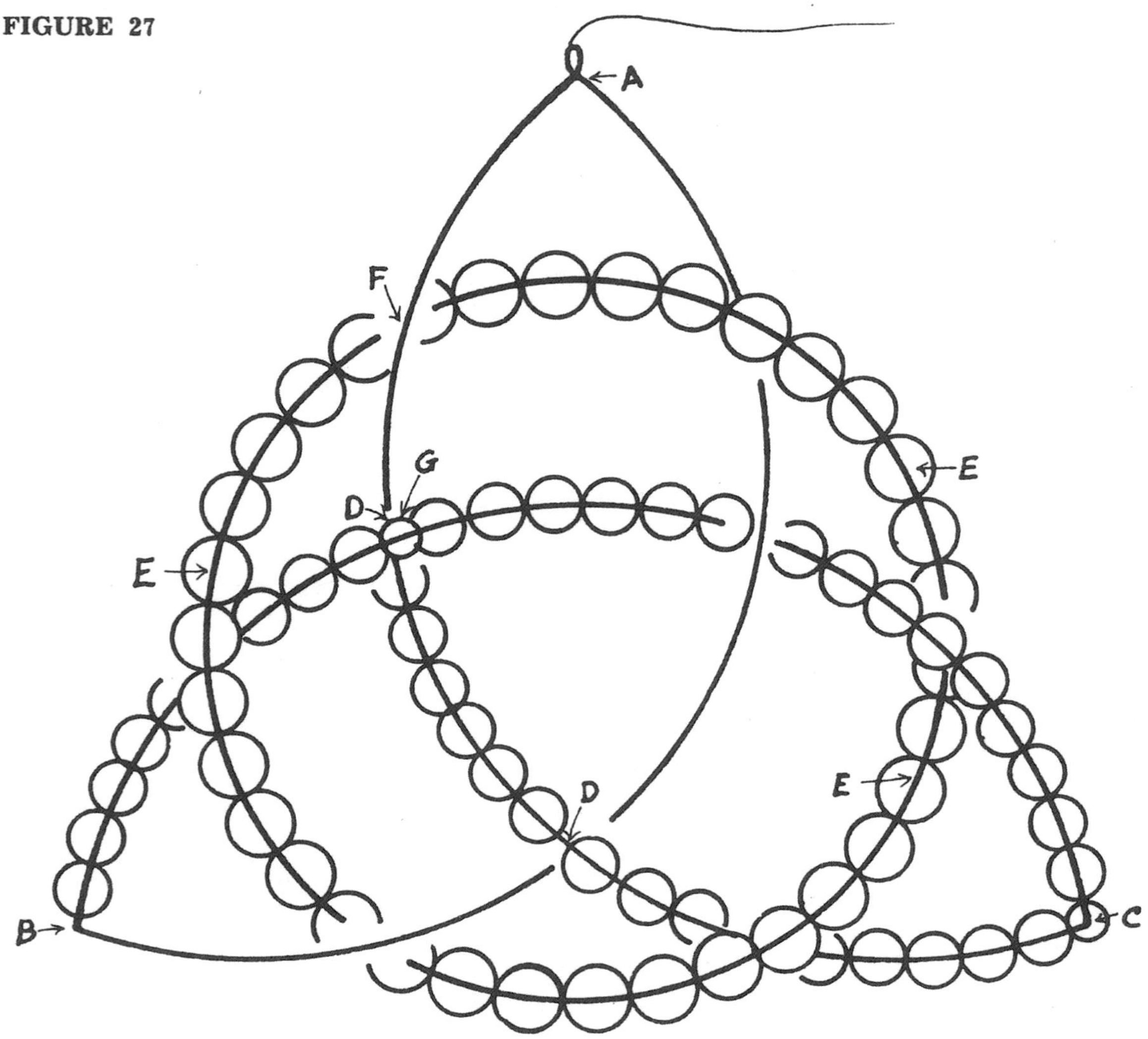

in each arc so that each side of the central triad equals each of the other sides.

For the circle, make a tiny loop in the end of a 16 inch length of #18 or #20 gold or copper colored wire. Shape the wire to the circle line, E on the pattern. String the wire circle with 10 mm gold glass beads. At the end, make another loop in the wire to fit over the first loop. Cut off the excess wire.

* * *

Shape the triquetra so that it will flow over and under the gold bead circle as it is shown on the pattern. It is simpler to make the circle, which is of easily broken glass beads, fairly flat and the triquetra, of relatively unbreakable pearls, undulating. With #30 wire, attach an 8 mm pearl to make the point at the end of the arc of the triquetra as shown at C. Fasten a pearl at each of the other two points. If necessary, wire a 6 or 8 mm pearl over the crossover D points to hide the attachment wires as shown at G.

Weave the gold circle in and out of the triquetra. Position the joining loops of the circle directly behind a wire of the triquetra, F. Wire the circle ends together with #30 wire. Use that same wire to fasten the F loops to the back of the triquetra. When the triquetra undulates properly over and under the circle, this attachment alone will hold the two figures in their relative positions. If it is desired, however, the circle may also be attached to the triquetra at several other points.

V. EPIPHANY (Five-Point) STAR & ROSE

FIGURE 28

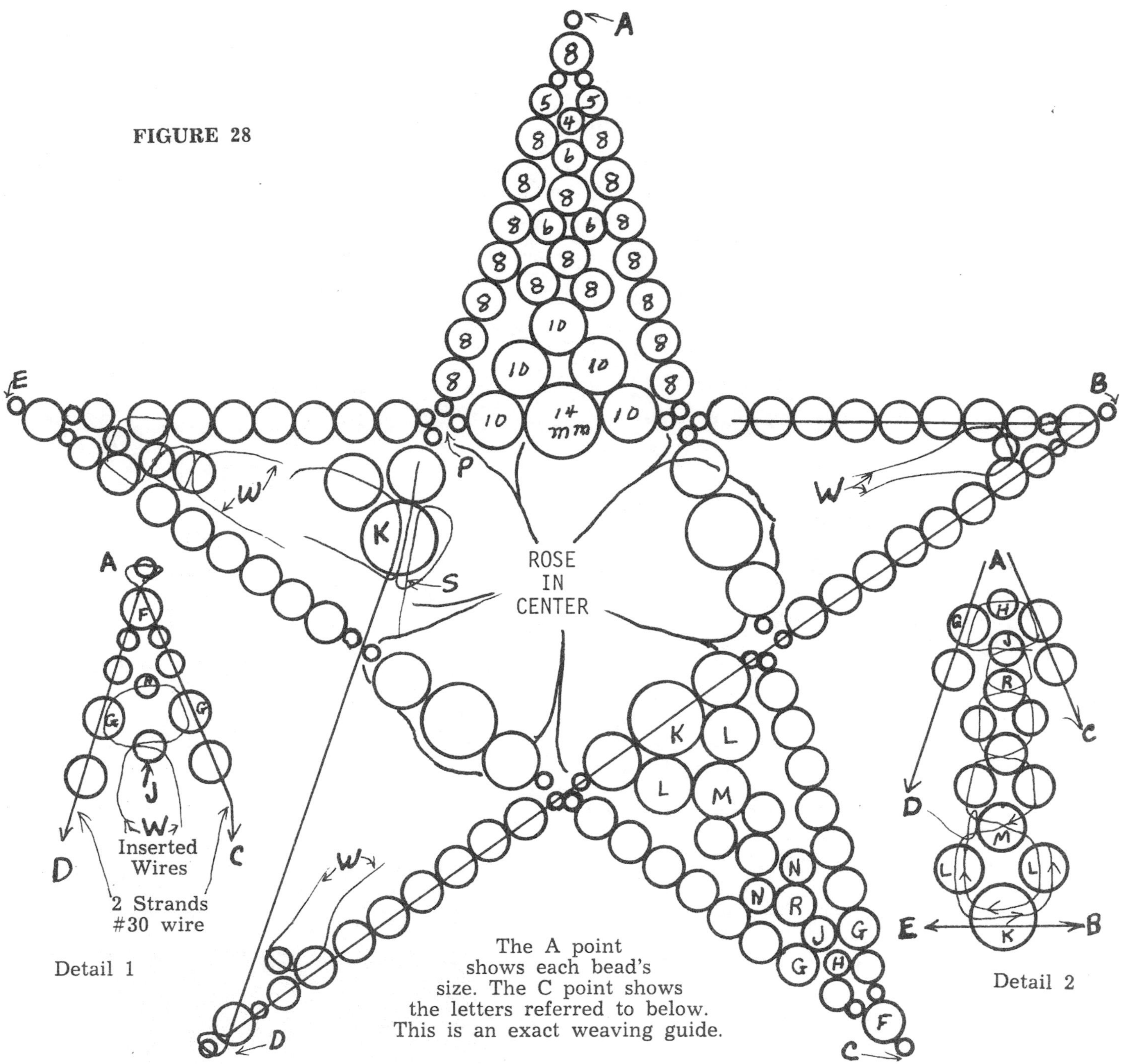

(Photographs on page 48 and on the back cover of Chrismons.)

The symbolism of the rose is derived from Isaiah's prophecy of Zion's glory, "The desert shall rejoice, and blossom as the rose." (35.1, K.J.) Because some people interpret this as a Messianic promise, the flower has come to symbolize the Messiah. In addition, the rose is a widely used figure for our Lord's mother Mary. This association led to its also becoming a symbol for Christ's human birth and His humanity.

On the other hand, the star points to Jesus' divinity. "Epiphany" is derived from a Greek word which means the appearance or revelation of a god. The Epiphany Star has five points; it specifically refers to the revelation or showing of our Savior as the Son of God. (Numbers 24:17; Matthew 2; Revelation 22:16.) Thus, a combination of the rose and the five-point star in one design is a portrayal of the two natures of the Christ: He is true God, and He is true Man.

Materials: Seed pearls; 4, 5, 6, 8, 10, and 14 mm pearls; #30 wire; metallic gold plated rose about 3″ in diameter. (The colors of this design may be reversed; the star may be gold metal beads, the rose white plastic. Or, the entire design may be either gold or white.) A comparison of the star on the back cover of *Chrismons* and the one on page 48 shows that the pearl weave inside the points may be varied to use the beads that are available.

Directions:

The basis of the star weave is rows of beads that follow the lines which are made when one draws a star in five strokes without taking the pencil from the paper. These lines may be seen on the Figure 28 pattern on page 47. Go from D to A to C to E to B to D. This stringing line is made of two strands of #30 wire. The beads that fill the peaks are woven on #30 wire pieces, W, which are inserted into the weave when the outline of the star is made.

* * *

Begin the weave at peak A with two 56 inch lengths of #30 wire. Unless otherwise instructed, handle these wires as one. String a seed bead on both wires 14 inches from one end of the wires. Run an 8 mm pearl, F, over the ends of all the wires. See Detail 1 on Figure 28. Push F tightly against the seed bead. Anchor the two 14 inch wire ends toward peak D, the two 42 inch ends toward C. On the D wires, string a seed bead, a 5 mm, and an 8 mm pearl G, in that order. Insert an extra 15 inch piece of #30 wire through G; bend the inserted wire, W, out of the way as shown at peak D on the pattern. On the AD wires string six 8 mm, two seed, a 10 mm and a 14 mm pearl in that order. At S, push the AD beads tight on the string; straight line anchor bead K temporarily.

On the two 42 inch wires toward C, string a seed, a 5 mm, and an 8 mm pearl, G. On the end of the W inserted wire toward point A, string a 4 mm pearl, H. Continue that end of the wire down through G toward the center of the star. Cross over both inserted wire ends in a 6 mm pearl, J. Anchor the inserted wires. (Detail 1.)

Continue to string the AC wires with six 8 mm, two seed, a 10 mm, a 14 mm, a 10 mm, two seed, and seven 8 mm pearls in that order. Insert a 12 inch W wire in the last strung 8 mm or G bead. On the AC wires, string a 5 mm, a seed, an 8 mm, and a seed pearl in that order. This is peak C. Push the beads tight on the AC wires; run the two wires back through bead F. The AC wires now become the CE wires. This is shown clearly at peak D on the pattern.

String the beads to make line CE like line AC. After peak E, string beads to point P on the AD line. At P, separate the two EB wires; lay one over and the other under the AD wires. On the B side of P, string a seed, a 10 mm, a 14 mm, a 10 mm, and a seed bead on both wires. Push the beads tight on the wires. Separate the wires to circle the AC wires. Then continue to bead the EB wire to peak B. Next bead the BD line. Remember to circle the previously strung lines at points P and to insert the W wires at each peak. Finally, string the line between D and S. At S, continue both wires through bead K. Pull the wires tight and anchor them.

* * *

Detail 2 on Figure 28 shows the weave inside each peak except E. After the W wires are crossed over in bead J, cross them over again in an 8 mm bead, R. Run a 6 mm pearl, N, on each wire; cross over the wires in an 8 mm pearl. Run each wire through an 8 mm pearl; cross over the wires in a 10 mm bead, M. Run a 10 mm pearl, L, on each wire. Then cross over the wires in the 14 mm K bead which is already woven on the line weave of the star. Backweave through the L and M beads and out the peak until the wires are anchored. Cut off the excess W wires.

On peak E, remove the temporary anchor from bead K so that the wires cross over in bead K at S. Weave the middle of peak E outward on these DA wires. First, put a 10 mm L bead on each pair of wires. Then cross over all the wires in a 10 mm M bead. Continue the weave through the next beads and beads N, R, J, G, and H. After H, twist the leftover wires together to make the hanger for the ornament. Continue to weave the W wires in peak E down through bead R and the next loop to anchor them. Cut off the excess W wires.

* * *

Run a needle threaded with #30 wire through the thick part of the stem just under the rose blossom. Run another #30 wire through the stem at right angles to the first wire. Set the rose in the hole at the center of the star. Wrap and twist the four pieces of #30 wire from the rose around the weaving wires of the pentagon at the middle of the star to hold the rose in place.

W. CROSS TRIUMPHANT or CROSS OF VICTORY

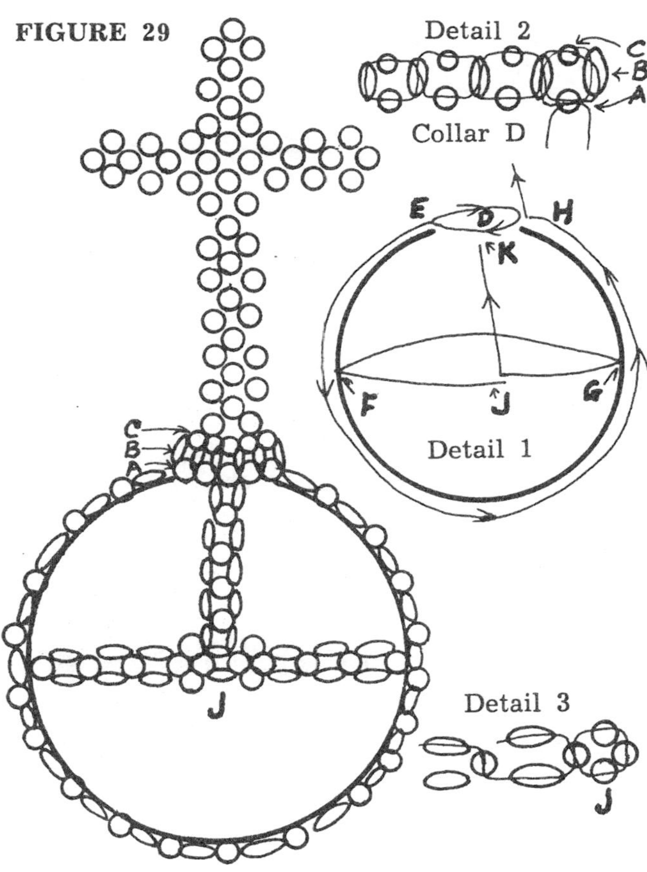

(Photograph on the front cover.)

A cross supreme over the world, which is represented by the ball, symbolizes the triumph of the Savior over the sin of the world. The divisions suggest continents which are united into one by the circular extension of the cross. Thus—the world united in Christ Who has dominion over all.

Materials: Gold stemmed (preferred) or Christmas tree ball, 2" to 4" in diameter. (Unbreakable plastic or metal balls are more durable than glass.) For the larger balls, 4 & 5 mm round pearls; for smaller balls, 3 & 4 mm pearls; for both sizes, 3 x 6 mm oval pearls; #30 hair wire.

Directions:

Remove the stem or cap from the ball. Molded plastic tops need not be taken off if they are smooth from top to bottom. Pearls are woven around the ball to form the design. Detail 1 of Figure 29 on this page shows how the design is made: First, a "collar," D and Detail 2, of beads is woven around the neck of the ball; the weave continues down from the collar at E to F, around the bottom of the ball, up to G, and on to H where it rejoins the collar. A new weave begins at J. When it circles the ball, it goes through the first weave at F and G. After the circle is closed at J, the weave goes up to join the collar at K. The weave continues through D to its top and across it to the back. The weave at H goes to the top of D, across D, and into the cross atop the ball.

Use of 4 and 5 mm pearls or 3 and 4 mm beads is a matter of preference. Generally, larger sizes suit larger balls; smaller sizes fit little balls. The directions call for 4 and 5 mm beads. On smaller balls, substitute 3 mm for the 4 mm beads and 4 mm for the 5 mm pearls.

* * *

Begin the weave on #30 wire, 36 inches plus three times the circumference of the ball long. A total length of 6 feet fits any ball. Center a 3 x 6 mm pearl on the wire. Run a 4 mm pearl over one end of the wire, a 5 mm pearl over the other end. Cross the wires over in another 3 x 6 mm oval. Continue the weave of 4 mm beads on the top (C on Detail 2 of Figure 29) lengthwise wires, 5 mm beads on the bottom (A on Detail 2) lengthwise wires, and 3 x 6 mm pearls (B on Detail 2) on the crossovers. When the weave fits the neck of the ball exactly, close the weave by crossing the wires over in the first 3 x 6 mm oval. This is the D collar. (If the ball has no stem, make a collar of six A beads only. Cross the wires over in the last (E) bead of the circle to close the collar.)

Continue the upper wire through the next top 4 mm bead, the 3 x 6 mm oval to the bottom of the weave, and back through the bottom 5 mm bead so that one wire extends from each side of the bottom E bead as shown on Detail 2.

Construction of this Chrismon requires careful and individual fitting of the weave to the ball. The fitted D collar may have from 6 to 11 beads in each A and C row as shown on Figure 30 below. Count the beads in the collar; match it to the ONE diagram on Figure 30 that contains the same number of beads. The E bead is the one from which the two wires extend. Mark the H and K beads on the design.

On the wires from E, make a straight weave of 3 x 6 mm lengthwise ovals and 5 mm crossover

FIGURE 30 Row A Collar Beads

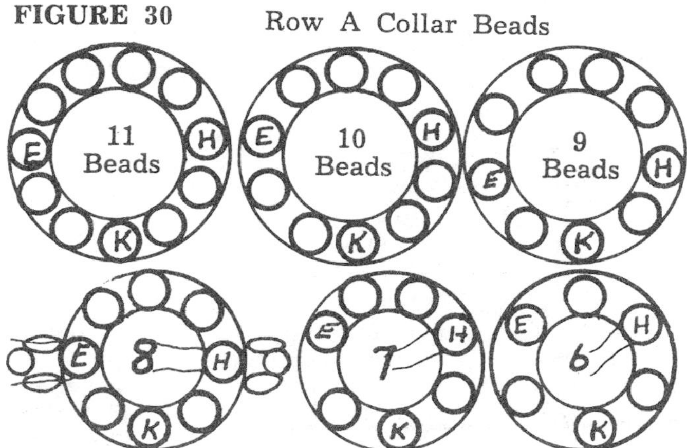

rounds. Go from E through F, around the bottom, up and through G to H. After the last lengthwise circle ovals, cross over the wires in the lower H bead; run each wire up through its adjoining 3 x 6 mm B oval; cross over the wires in the top H bead on row C. Fold the wires; fasten them out of the way with a tie twist.

(It is easier to weave the "cage" when it is off the ball, but fit the cage to the ball frequently. While the directions call for 3 x 6 mm ovals on the lengthwise wires, 5 mm beads may be substituted in some loops to shorten the weave for an exact fit to the ball. Such loops must be on both sides of the circle to balance it.)

Place the cage on the ball. Mark loops F and G on the vertical circle; each bisects the circle equally from top to bottom and is the same distance from the collar. Begin the horizontal circle at J on a length of #30 wire, five times the circumference of the ball. If desired, the first loop may be of 5 mm beads only as seen on Detail 3 of Figure 29. Continue the weave of 3 x 6 mm ovals on the lengthwise and 5 mm rounds on the crossover wires to and through the F loop. (At F, the crossovers are the previously woven 3 x 6 mm ovals; the lengthwise beads, the already woven 5 mm rounds.) Continue the weave of the horizontal circle around the back of the ball, to and through G, and around to J.

At J, cross over the wires in the first bead. Run the upper wire through the first top lengthwise bead; run the bottom wire through the first lower lengthwise bead, up through the second crossover, and through the top lengthwise bead from left to right. The wires are now in position to weave up the front from J to K. At K, cross over the wires in the lower collar K bead and run each up through its adjacent oval. Cross them over in the upper K bead.

Figure 31 below shows how beads are woven to close the top of all except the 6 bead collars.

FIGURE 31 Beads woven atop and in the center of the collar on wires from the top K crossover.

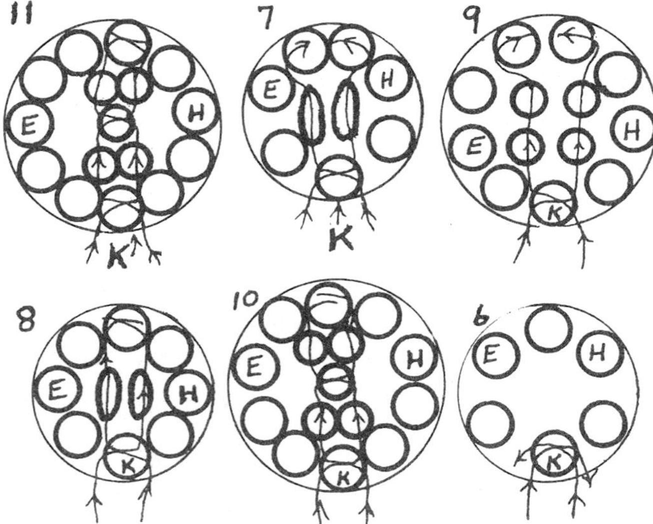

(When only 6 beads are in row C, backweave the K wires to anchor them; cut off their excess.) Select the ONE pattern on Figure 31 that has the same number of beads as the woven collar. Follow that pattern to weave beads on the wires from bead K at the front of the collar to the back. (Beads are either 5 mm rounds or 3 x 6 mm ovals.) After the wires are run through the proper bead at the back of the collar, backweave to anchor them; cut off the excess wire.

* * *

Weave the cross arms of all 5 mm beads or of 5 mm round crossovers and 3 x 6 mm lengthwise ovals. In the latter case, make all the center loop beads 5 mm rounds. When the first bead is included, the cross arms have 8 crossovers. Back weave the arm to anchor the beads; cut off the excess wire.

FIGURE 32 Cross base woven on wires from the collar top H crossover.

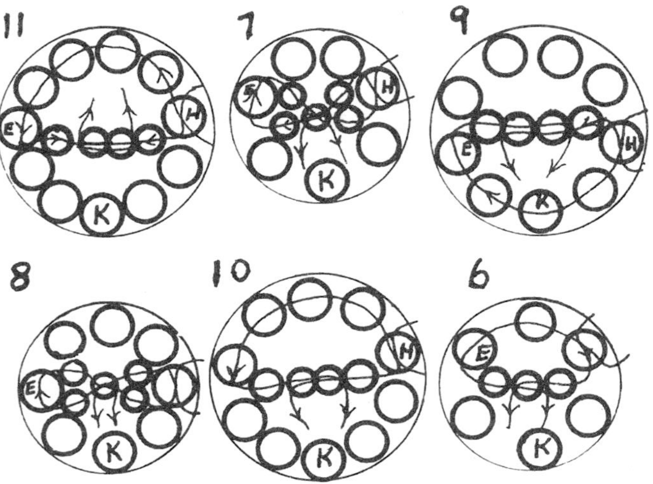

Figure 32 above diagrams the beads that form the cross base from the top H bead. All are 5 mm pearls. Note that, on those collars with 7 or 8 beads, a bead is strung on each wire that emerges from bead H. After another bead is run on both wires, one wire is beaded both before and after it crosses over in the top E bead. Then that wire goes back through the center bead.

On the other collars, one wire from H is run through several top collar beads to a point opposite the wire that remains at H. Then each wire is beaded to the center beads in which the wires cross over. Follow the weaving lines and beads on the pattern that matches the number of beads in the collar that is woven.

The last beads on any pattern on Figure 32 are crossovers. From these crossovers, weave the cross upright, the beads of which should match the arm weave. After the 6th pair of lengthwise beads after the base crossover, weave through the cross arms. Continue to weave three more crossovers on the upright. Twist the leftover wires together to make the hanger.

X. CROWN

(Photograph on page 64.)

The crown is a symbol for the Kingship of our Lord, Jesus Christ, the King of kings and Lord of lords. I Timothy 6:15. This device may also evoke thoughts of our Savior's victory over sin and the death of the cross and His place of honor at the right hand of God. I Corinthians 15:54 ff.

A congregation in Virginia reported this incident: At a children's service, one of the young participants made her own addition to the program. She walked to the Chrismon tree, took off her costume crown, and placed it on the tree. Then she wandered to the creche to look at the baby—to see if the baby understood?

Materials: 6 mm gold glass beads; gold seed or rocaille beads; 3 mm gold metal beads; 4 mm, 5 mm, and 5 x 7 mm pearls; 5 mm and 8 mm gold cup and 18 mm gold sunburst sequins; #18 or #20 gold or copper colored wire; #30 wire; white chenille stems, white glue.

Directions:

Construction of the crown may seem involved, but it is easy if the wiring diagrams on Figure 33 on this page below are carefully followed. In fact, many people could make the crown merely by studying and following the diagrams and ignoring the written explanations. Once the general method is understood, construction goes rapidly.

Although these directions call for 6 mm gold glass beads, glass beads from 6 to 10 mm may be used. If the larger sizes are wanted, work out an arrangement in which the finished crown is about three inches high with a headband about five inches in diameter. If glass beads molded in units of three beads can be obtained, use them to weave the "diamonds" that form the crown. Such beads make for more precise peaks.

Figure 33 shows, at the left, how the wires are run through the beads and the number and position of the beads. As the pattern moves toward the right, additional wires and beads are

FIGURE 33

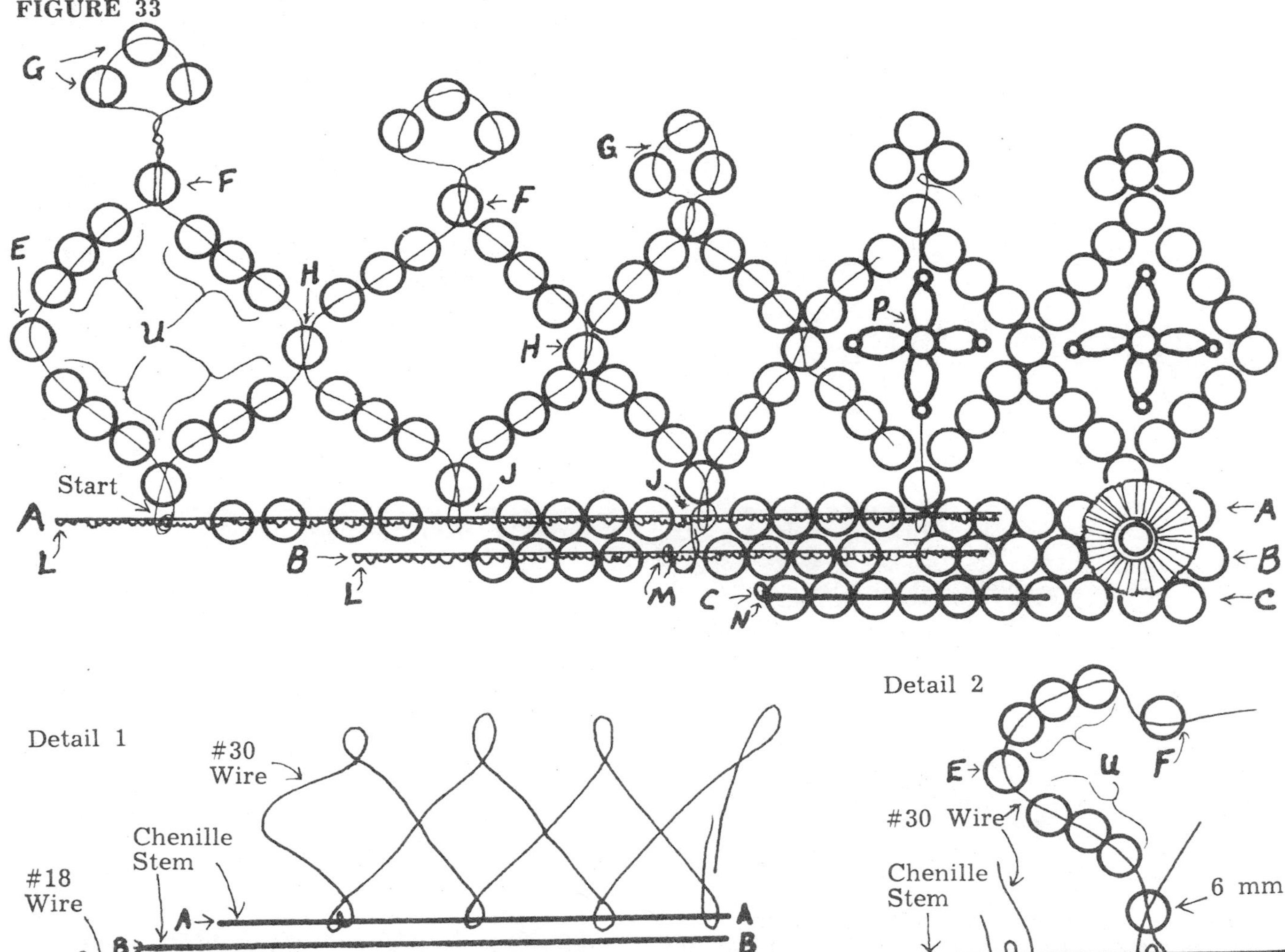

added to complete the crown. The extreme right shows a finished section of the crown in its actual size. Detail 1 of Figure 33 names the wires used to make the crown and diagrams their relative positions.

* * *

Shape a twelve inch chenille stem, B on Figure 33, as far as it will go around a five inch diameter circle. String 6 mm gold glass beads on the stem in groups of four. Begin the beads about one inch from the end of the stem; allow about 3/16 of an inch space between each group of four beads. At the end of the stem, add another stem and continue to bead it until a total of 12 groups of four, each separated from the next by about 3/16 inch space, are on the wires. Fasten the stems together to close the five inch diameter circle. Mark the two places on the circle where the stems are pieced.

If single beads are used, the chenille stems are joined by wrapping #30 wire tightly around both the new and old stems in the 3/16 inch of space between the groups of four beads. If beads molded in groups of three make the peaks, use a group of three and a single bead to make a group of four at the junction of two stems. Cut off the stems so that they cross over in the three bead unit. In this situation, the stems need not be wired together. Twist a piece of wire around the places on the circle where the stems are joined to mark those points.

Bend a tiny loop at the end of a 20 inch length of #18 or #20 gold or copper colored wire. Shape the wire to the five inch circle. String 6 mm gold glass beads on the wire to fill the five inch circle. Make another tiny loop at the end of the #18 wire to match the first loop. This circle C should exactly match the size of circle B on chenille stems, but, since no 3/16 inch spaces are made, circle C will contain more beads than circle B.

Begin circle A on a chenille stem bent to a five inch circle in the same manner as circle B. Twist the middle of a 72 inch length of #30 wire tightly around the stem one inch from the end of the stem. See "start" on Figure 33 and the #30 and A wires on Details 1 and 2. (A shorter #30 wire may be used. In that case the #30 wires must be replaced when they run out. End short wires and add new ones by twisting the new and old wires tightly around the 3/16 inch space between the groups of four 6 mm beads on chenille stem A.)

Run a 6 mm bead over both ends of the #30 wire. On one wire only, string eight more 6 mm beads. (If glass beads in units of three are used, the U's on Figure 33 and its Detail 2 show where they are placed.) String three more beads for peak G as diagramed on Figure 33. (While the beads are shown loosely strung to illustrate the weave, they must be strung tightly so that the finished shape looks like the beads at the right of Figure 33.) Run the #30 wire back through bead F. Hold the wire firmly and twist the top three beads so that the wires twist around each other to hold the top beads in the position shown on peak G. String three more beads (or one unit of three 6 mm beads) over each #30 wire end. Cross over the wires in another 6 mm bead, H. Tighten the wires; anchor them. Shape the first peak to the diamond pattern. (To have a firm crown, it MUST be shaped as it is woven, not after the whole A circle is complete.)

String four 6 mm beads on the A chenille stem. Run a unit of three (or three individual beads) and one more 6 mm bead on the bottom wire from H on Figure 33. Then twist the wire to hold around the A stem in the 3/16 inch space between the groups of four beads. Run the #30 wire from A back through the last strung 6 mm bead.

On the upper wire from H, string a unit of three 6 mm beads and one 6 mm bead. Add the three individual 6 mm beads to make peak H. After running back through the second F bead, twist the peak to hold. Run three 6 mm beads on the wire. String three 6 mm beads on the lower #30 wire. Cross over both wires in a 6 mm bead, the second H.

Continue to bead the two #30 wires and the A stem until twelve groups of four beads each are on the chenille circle A. Circle A is pieced in the same way as circle B. With a twist of wire, mark the places where the stems are pieced. Frequently check the beading and shape of circle A against the previously woven circle B. Both must be the same size and have the same spacing between the groups of four beads.

After the 6 mm bead at the base of the twelfth diamond is strung, twist the #30 wire around stem A and leave the wire in that position. After the twelfth peak is beaded on the other #30 wire, string the three beads on that same wire to make the upper right of the diamond. Then run that same #30 wire down through the E bead of the first diamond to close the diamond weave. Continue the #30 wire through three more 6 mm beads to make the lower right edge of the diamond and through the 6 mm bead at the base of the diamond to the chenille stem A. Twist the wire around chenille stem A to anchor it with the other #30 wire.

Position the crown woven on circle A atop stem circle B. The 3/16 inch spaces must be directly over each other; the two circles must also be placed so that pieced stems are over or under unbroken sections of the other stemmed circle. See points L. Temporarily fasten the circles together at four points with pipe cleaners.

Place the beaded #18 wire circle C under circle B in such a position that the joining point of C is under solid sections of circles A and B. See N on Figure 33. Wrap pipe cleaner pieces around C and B and A to join them temporarily.

* * *

String the cross at the center of each diamond on a 24 inch length of #30 wire. Center a gold seed bead on the wire. Run a 5 x 7 mm

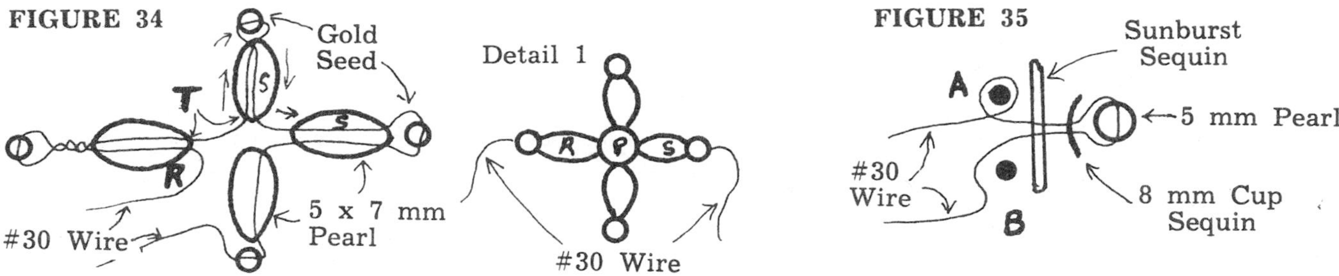

pearl over both wire ends. Push the pearl tight against the seed bead. Spread the wires to anchor them. See R on Figure 34 on this page above. String another 5 x 7 pearl and a seed bead on one of the wires. Run the wire back through the pearl as shown by the arrows around bead S. Tighten the wires so that the pearls touch at the T corners. String the third extension, S, and the fourth arm in the same way. Continue the wire through the first oval R. Anchor the wire to hold the cross in place.

String a 3 mm gold bead, P on Figure 33, over the remaining wire at the center of the cross. Then run the wire through the hole in the middle of the wires at the cross center. Tighten the wire to pull bead P against the center of the cross. String another 3 mm gold bead on the wire. Run the wire back through the center of the cross. Tighten the wire so that the bead is at the center of the cross and on the side opposite the first gold bead. Run the #30 wire at the center through oval S; the wires now extend from opposite arms of the cross as shown on Detail 1 of Figure 34.

Run the shorter wire from the cross through bead F atop the diamond. Twist the #30 wire around the wires from atop bead F to anchor the cross at the center of the diamond. Continue the #30 wire through a lower peak bead. String a 5 mm pearl on the wire. Run the wire, from front to back through the center of the three bead peak; wrap the wire around a peak bead to hold. Cut off the excess wire.

Run the longer #30 wire from the cross through the bottom diamond bead to stem A. After the #30 wire is tightly wrapped to hold around stem A, string an 18 mm gold sunburst sequin, an 8 mm gold cup sequin, and a 4 mm pearl on the #30 wire outside the headband. See Figure 35 on this page above. Run the wire back through the sequins and between rows A and B to inside the headband. Tighten the wire so that the pearl centered sequins are against the band beads and cover the 3/16 inch spaces on the outside of the headband.

Wrap the #30 wire around the space on stem B to hold the sequins in place. See M on Figure 33. Then wrap the wire in a figure 8 around the #18 wire between the beads on row C and row B. Cut off the excess wire.

On every third peak, do NOT cut off the excess wire at the headband. Instead, lace the wire in and out of the B and A rows to the bottom bead of the diamond. Wrap the #30 wire tightly around the two #30 wires that go into the bottom of the base 6 mm bead. Fasten the leftover #30 wire loosely around the peak to hold it out of the way temporarily.

After crosses are in all the diamonds, glue a 5 mm gold cup sequin to cover each exposed stem space inside the headband. Loosen the leftover wires from each third peak. Twist the wires together at the center of the crown about half an inch below its top so that the crown hangs straight. Let one wire extend up as the hanger.

Home Size:

The home size crown of 6 mm gold glass beads only is a simplified version of the full size design. The headband is one 12 inch chenille stem strung with 12 groups of three 6 mm beads. Spaces between the bead groups are 1/8 inch long. Join the circle by crossing the ends of the stem in a group of three beads into which glue is run before the stems are inserted.

Twist the middle of a 60 inch length of #30 wire to hold around one of the spaces in the chenille stem. Follow the weaving procedure of the full size design but use the number of 6 mm beads shown on the homesize pattern on Figure 36 on this page below. Note especially that the peak on Figure 36 has only one bead, G. After G is strung, the bead is turned so that the wires into and out of G twist on themselves to hold.

After the weave of 12 diamonds is complete, twist the end of a 9 inch piece of #30 wire around the wires below the lowest bead of each third diamond. Twist the wires together at the center of the crown to make a hanger. Glue 5 mm gold cup sequins to cover the bare stems on both the inside and the outside of the headband.

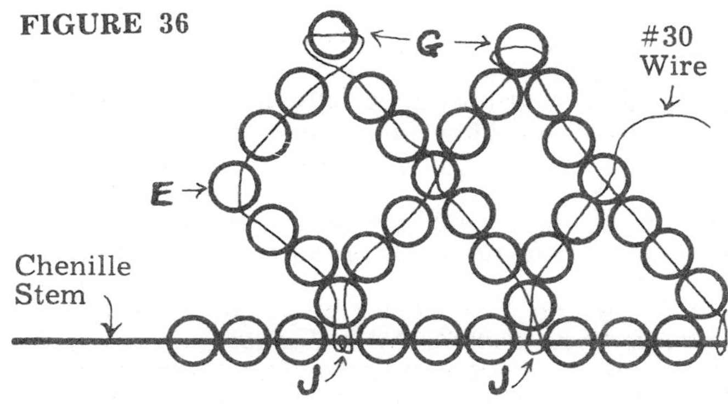

Y. CROSS IN ETERNITY

(Photograph at the right.)

Once in history, God,
through His Son, Jesus,
made Himself known to man
and provided for
man's eternal salvation.
By the inspiration
of the Spirit of God
every person can walk
with God eternally.
Let men, women, children,
let all believe and
accept the one sacrifice
that was made
. . . for all time.

Materials: 10 & 16 mm gold glass beads; gold seed beads; about 10 mm white iris shamrock sequins; 5 mm gold cup sequins; 12" white chenille stems; #30 wire; gold beading wire; white glue.

Directions:

To begin the cross place a 10 mm gold glass bead 8 inches from the end of a 20 inch length of #30 wire. Hold the wires close to the bead in one hand; with the other hand, turn the bead so that the wires twist on themselves to hold the bead in place. See Detail 1 of Figure 37 on this page below. Run another 10 mm bead over both wires; push it against the first bead. About 1/8 inch from the second bead, twist both wires to hold around a 2½ inch piece of chenille stem ¾ inch from one end of the stem. String two 10 mm beads on one wire; run that wire back through the first bead to the stem. Turn the end bead so that the arm matches the first arm. Wrap the wire around the stem to hold. See Detail 2 of Figure 37.

Lay the longer #30 wire along the stem toward C on Detail 3 of the pattern. String two 10 mm beads over the #30 wire and the stem. Straight line anchor the last bead with the #30 wire so that the bead next to the crucial point of the cross is 1/8 inch from the center. In like manner, string four 10 mm beads over the other #30 wire and stem toward D.

Shape a 12 inch chenille stem to circle E on Figure 37. The ends will lap over each other. String sixteen 16 mm beads on the center of the stem. Push each end of the chenille stem into the beads on the other end of the stem to close the circle. If beads with large holes are preselected for the ends of the circle, this procedure is easier. Push and work the stem ends and the beads until the bead circle is closed. Only enough space should be between the beads so that a piece of #30 wire can be wrapped around the chenille

FIGURE 37

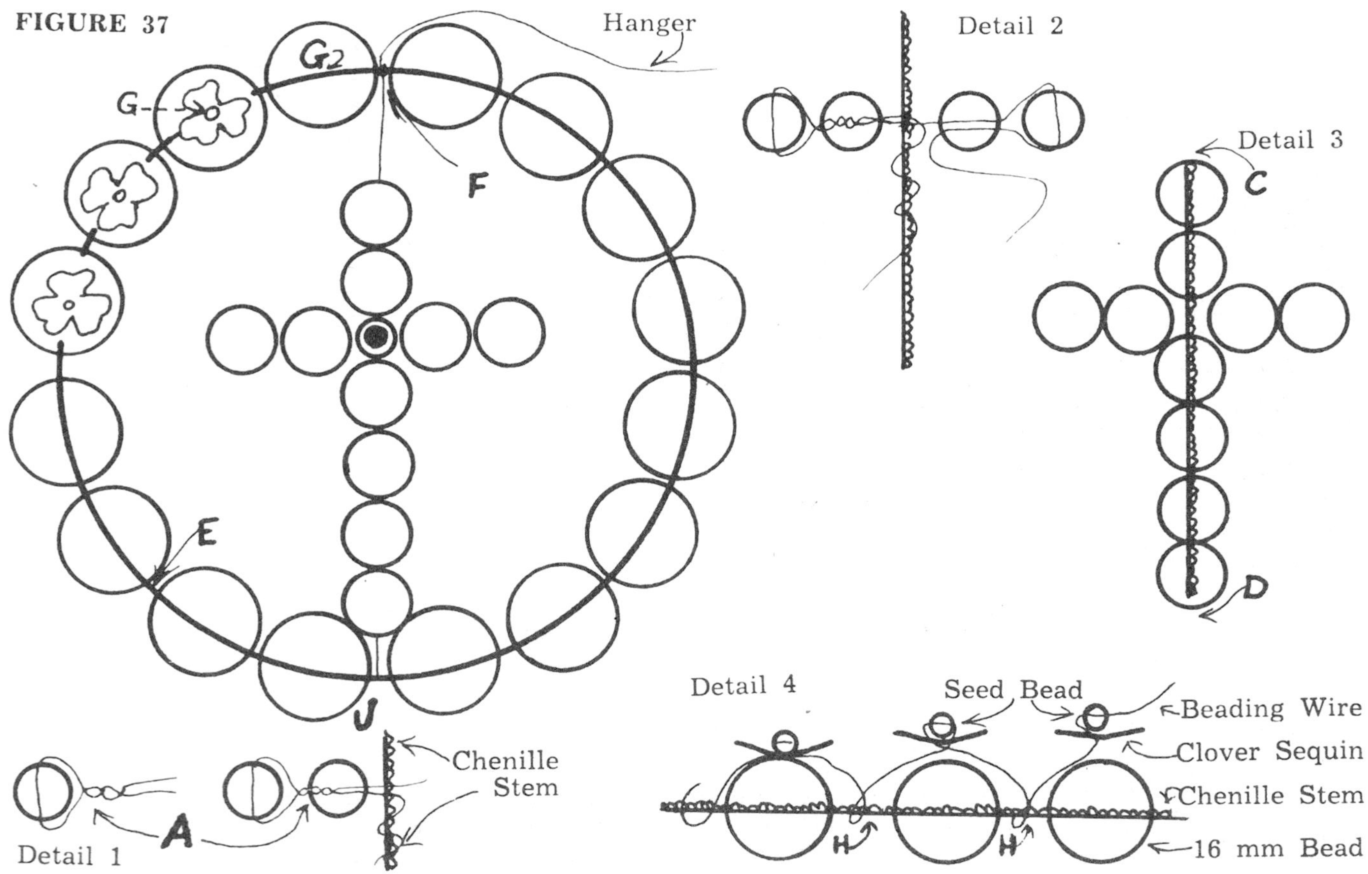

stem. Tightly wrap the end of a 24 inch length of beading wire around the middle of the crossed over wires to hold them in place. This is point F on the pattern.

Cut off the short end of the beading wire at F. Follow Detail 4 of Figure 37 to weave a shamrock atop each 16 mm circle bead on the long end of the beading wire from F. Run a 10 mm white iris clover (shamrock) sequin and a gold seed bead over the beading wire. Run the wire back through the sequin. Position the bead centered sequin at G, the center top of the first bead. Tighten the wire. Lay it closely against the bead down to the stem. Carry the wire inside the circle, under the stem, and up on the outside of the stem. Then thread the end of the beading wire under the previously laid wire at H. (This maneuver keeps the shamrocks centered atop the beads.) Pull the wires tight. Wire a sequin atop each bead until all the circle beads are covered. Cut off the excess wire.

To set the cross in the circle, twist the #30 wire from the leg of the cross around the stem at J to hold the cross next to the circle. Cut off the excess #30 wire. Twist the wire from the top of the cross to hold around the chenille stem at F. The leftover wire is the hanger. Glue a 5 mm gold sequin to cover the wires on each side of the crucial point of the cross.

Z. TRIANGLE & TREFOIL

(Photograph on this page below.)

Two geometric figures, a trefoil and an equilateral triangle combine to define the Godhead. The triangle, one of the oldest and most common symbols for the Triune, has three distinct parts united into a perfect whole. The trefoil, also of three equal parts, is a modification of three interlaced circles which suggest the eternal nature of the three Persons.

Materials: 4 & 6 mm pearls; 16 mm gold glass beads; 12" chenille stems; #30 wire; white thread; #18 or #14 green florist wire.

Directions:

Center a 6 mm pearl, A on Figure 38 and its Detail 1 on page 56, on two 24 inch lengths of #30 wire. Run the two wires from one side through a 4 mm pearl, the two wires on the other side through another 4 mm pearl. Anchor each pair of wires.

Follow the Detail 1 pattern to weave the corner and legs of the triangle. Weave each leg to bead L on Figure 38, one bead short of the middle M bead. Count the beads in the pattern; notice the size of each. Weave the other two corners and legs to L in the same way. Place the woven corners and legs over the pattern; select two leg pieces to join. Add the M beads by crossing the wires from beads L over in the M beads; two wires are in each M bead. Continue to weave one pair of wires through a previously woven loop or two of the opposite leg pieces to anchor the wires. Cut off the leftover wires. Close each of the other legs in the same way.

* * *

Bend a 36 inch piece of #14 florist wire to follow line T on the pattern. While the pattern shows only two sides of line T, continue the wire to make a triangle. Let the ends lap over each other about two inches. (If eighteen inch #18 wire is used, make the triangle of two pieces. Begin one piece at D on the AC line. Shape the wire to and around A, to and around B, and to and around C. Begin the other piece at D on line BC. Go to and around C, to and around A, and to and around B. Wrap #30 wire around the angles to fasten the two pieces together.

Place the florist wire behind the woven pearl triangle. Fasten the two together by looping white thread around the green wire and the wires of the woven pearls.

* * *

Shape three chenille stems, E on the pattern, to the P to P line. Join two stems from points J to P by wrapping #30 wire tightly around them from J to P. Place a 16 mm gold glass bead over the stem ends; let the #30 wire come out of the bead hole at P. Carry the #30 wire around the bead to one of the stems. Twist the #30 wire around the stem to hold the bead in place. See K on the pattern.

Run 16 mm gold glass beads on one of the stems to the next J point. Attach another stem from points J to P. Continue to bead the stems until the trefoil is complete except for one PJ

FIGURE 38

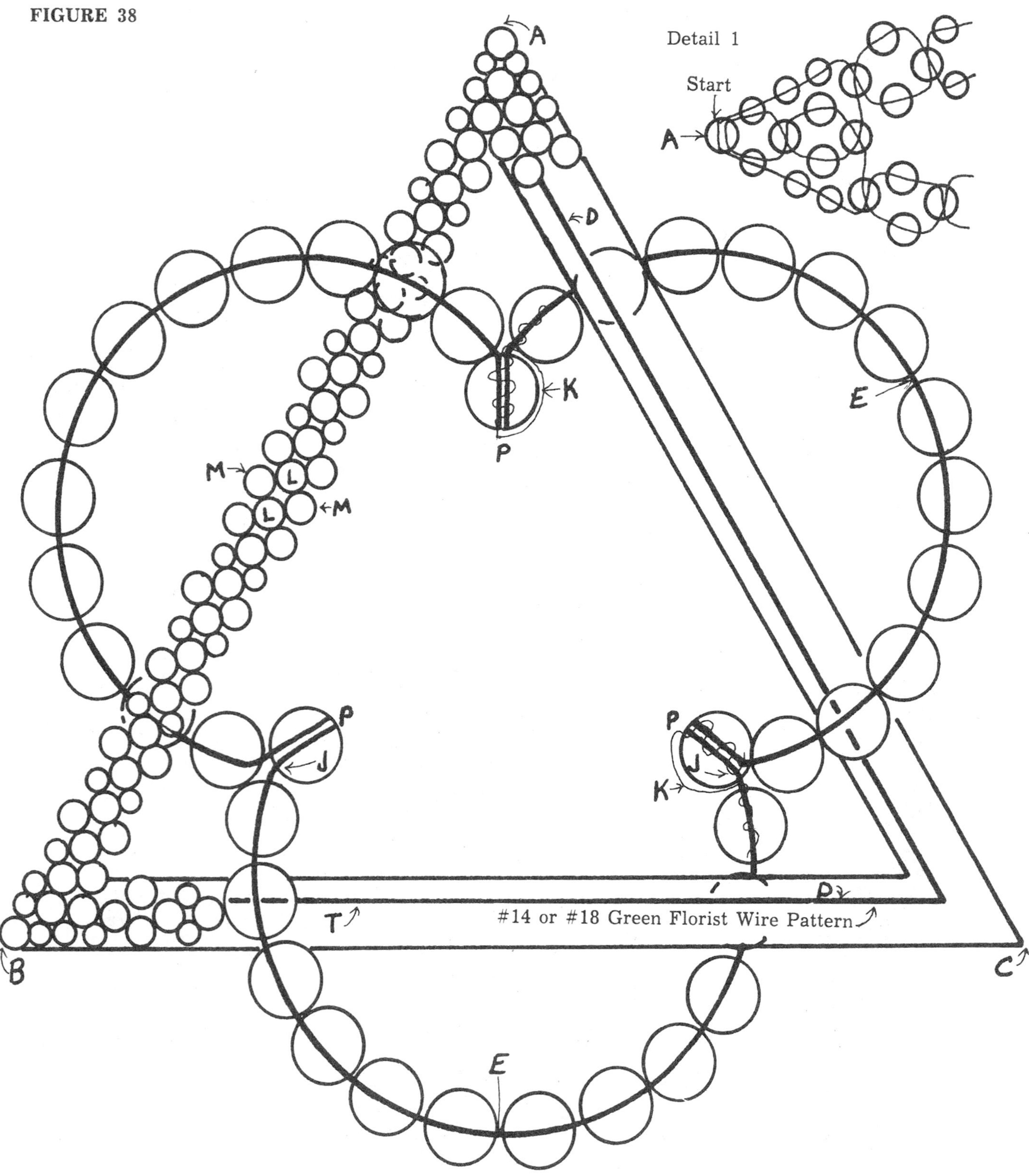

closing point.

Lace the trefoil into and over and under the triangle as shown on the pattern and picture. Wire the last trefoil point closed at PJ. Shape both the triangle and the trefoil so that they pass over and under each other smoothly. With pieces of #30 wire, fasten the trefoil to the triangle at each intersecting point. Run #30 wire through the hole just under the top bead to serve as the hanger.

AA. CHI & CROSS WOVEN THROUGH TWO CIRCLES

(Photograph on page 58 at the left.)

This ancient design suggests the Christ Who died on the cross at a specific time in history. (The outer circle represents the finite.) Yet this same Christ provided, by means of that death, the eternal answer (the inner circle, the infinite) that goes beyond life into eternity.

Materials: 1¼" wide gold vinyl festooning or wide, thick gold tinsel; 8 & 16 mm gold glass beads; 5 mm pearls; ornamental gold sequins about 8 to 16 mm in diameter; stranded (cable type) wire about 1/8" in diameter; white chenille stems; #30 wire.

FIGURE 39

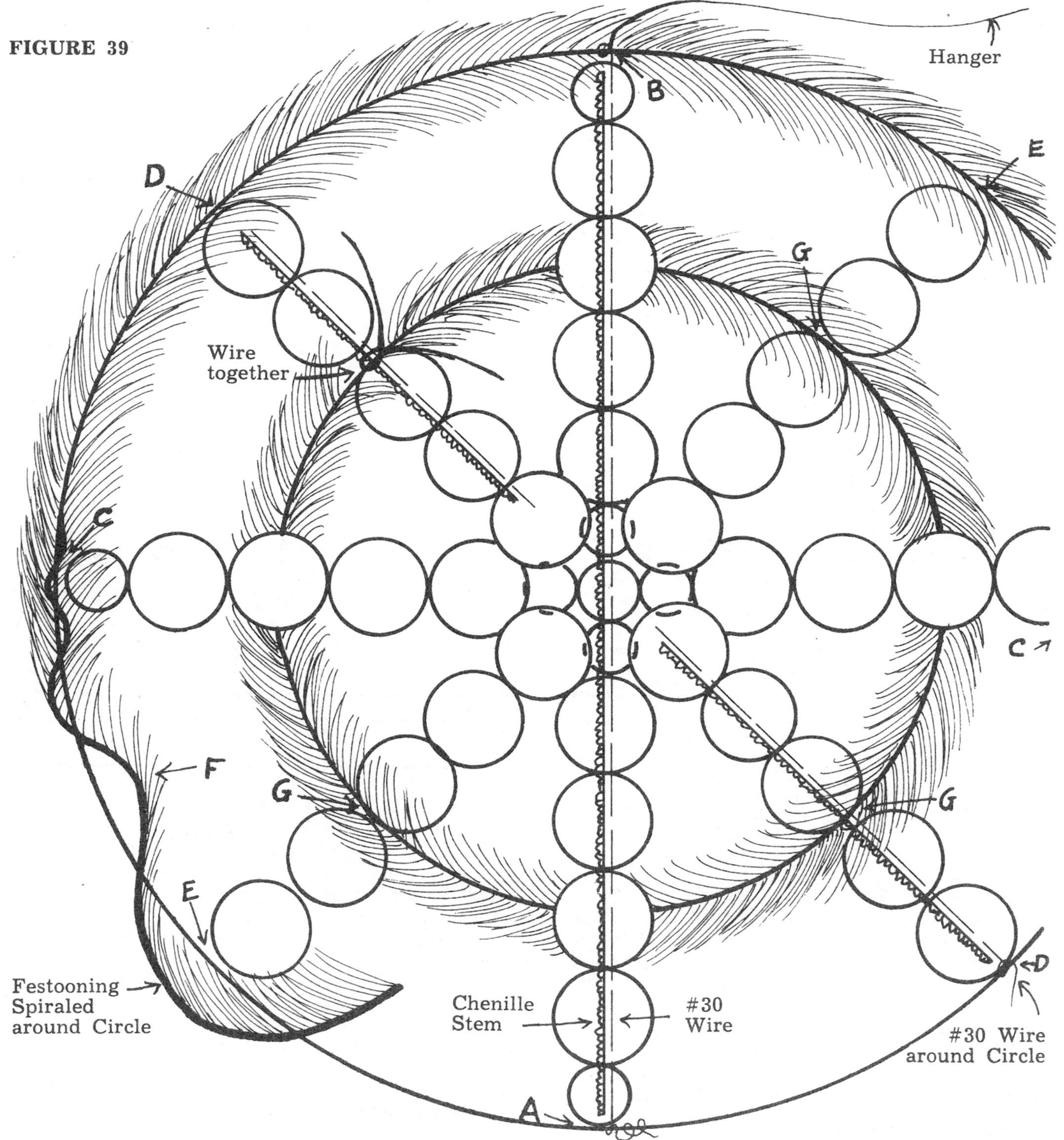

Directions:

Covering Stranded Wire with Festooning

Shape the one-eighth inch thick stranded wire circles. Use a 16 inch length for the inner 4½ inch diameter circle and 26 inches for the larger 7½ inch ring. Twist the wire around itself at the ends to hold the circle closed.

Cover each circle with 1¼ inch gold vinyl festooning. Cut wider fringes to the 1¼ inch width. Attach the solid edge of a piece of fringe to the circle with glue, tape, and/or wire. (This is done most easily at the joint where two wires are twisted on each other.) See F on the Figure 39 pattern on page 57. Spiral the festooning around the circle by winding the solid edge around the wire circle while the cut edge flares out over the previously placed solid edge. After the circle is covered, twist #30 wire around the solid edge to hold it in place. With a needle, lift and pull out pieces of fringe that have been caught by the wires. With scissors, trim off any fringe that is out of line so that the circle is a neat ring no more than one inch wide at its thickest. If the circle is too fuzzy, the design is lost.

* * *

For the cross upright, lay a 20 inch piece of #30 wire beside a 7¼ inch chenille stem. String one 8 mm, four 16 mm, two 8 mm, four 16 mm, and one 8 mm gold glass beads in that order over both wires. Attach the beaded stem to the circle by twisting the #30 wire from one end around the outer fringed circle to hold at A. Tighten the #30 wire out of the top of the stem; twist it around the outer circle at B. Leftover wire at B is the hanger. Bead another stem and #30 wire in the same manner. Fasten it to the outer circle to form the CC arm beam of the cross. Note the separation of beads at the crucial point to allow the wires to pass over each other. Lay the inner circle under the cross.

For the Chi, string each of two 7½ inch stems and 14 inch lengths of #30 wire with ten 16 mm gold glass beads. Separate the beads in the middle so that five are on each side. Insert the DD section of the Chi over the crucial point of the cross and under the inner circle. Flatten the DD line to flow smoothly over the inner circle. Pull the #30 wire that extends out of each end of the DD line to tighten the row of beads. Twist the #30 wires around the outer circle to hold the line of beads in place. Attach the EE line of the Chi in the same manner. Cut off the excess wires from the DD and the EE lines.

If desired, twist #30 wire around the inner circle wire and the Chi stems to hold the circle to the Chi. Wire a gold ornamental sequin to cover the wires on each side of the crucial point. Center the sequin with a 5 mm pearl if it is wanted. With a needle, pull out any pieces of fringe that may be caught in the wires at points A, B, C, D, E, and G.

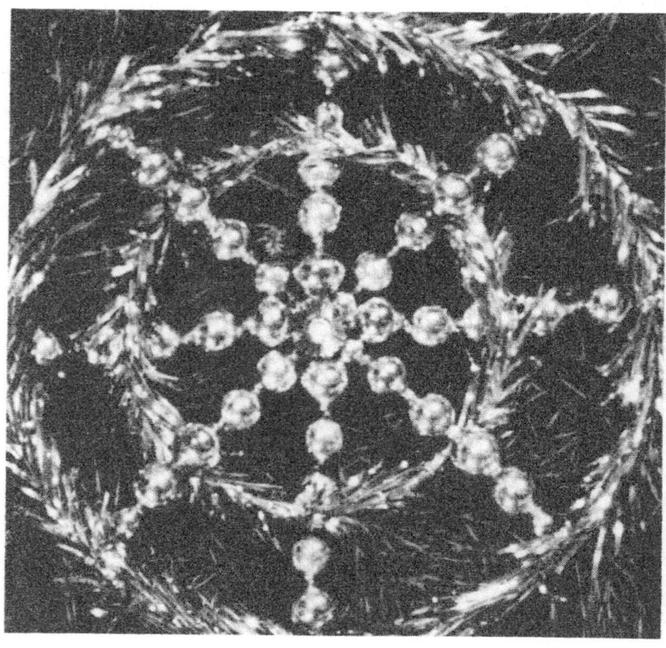

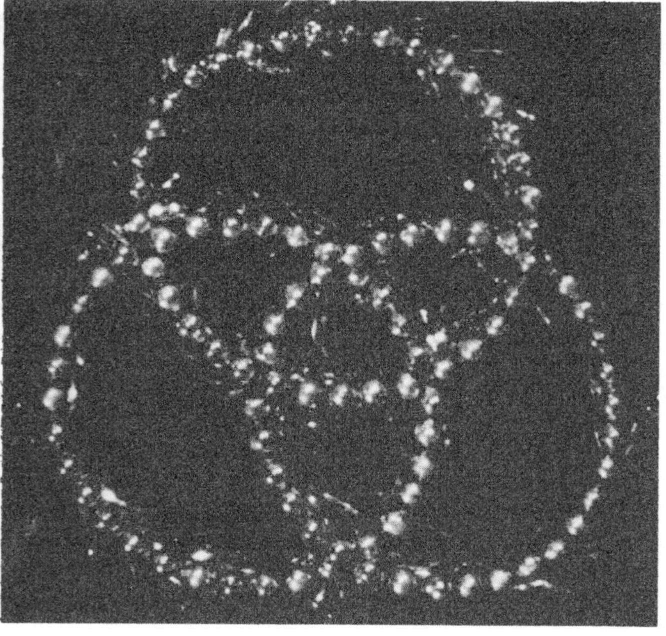

BB. THREE ENTWINED CIRCLES

(Photograph on this page above at the right.)

A symbol for the Holy Trinity, one God in three Persons, Each eternal, All One.

Materials: 10 mm gold glass beads; 1¼″ gold vinyl festooning; 1/8″ stranded wire; #30 wire; #18 or #20 gold or copper colored wire.

Directions:

From one-eighth inch diameter stranded

FIGURE 40

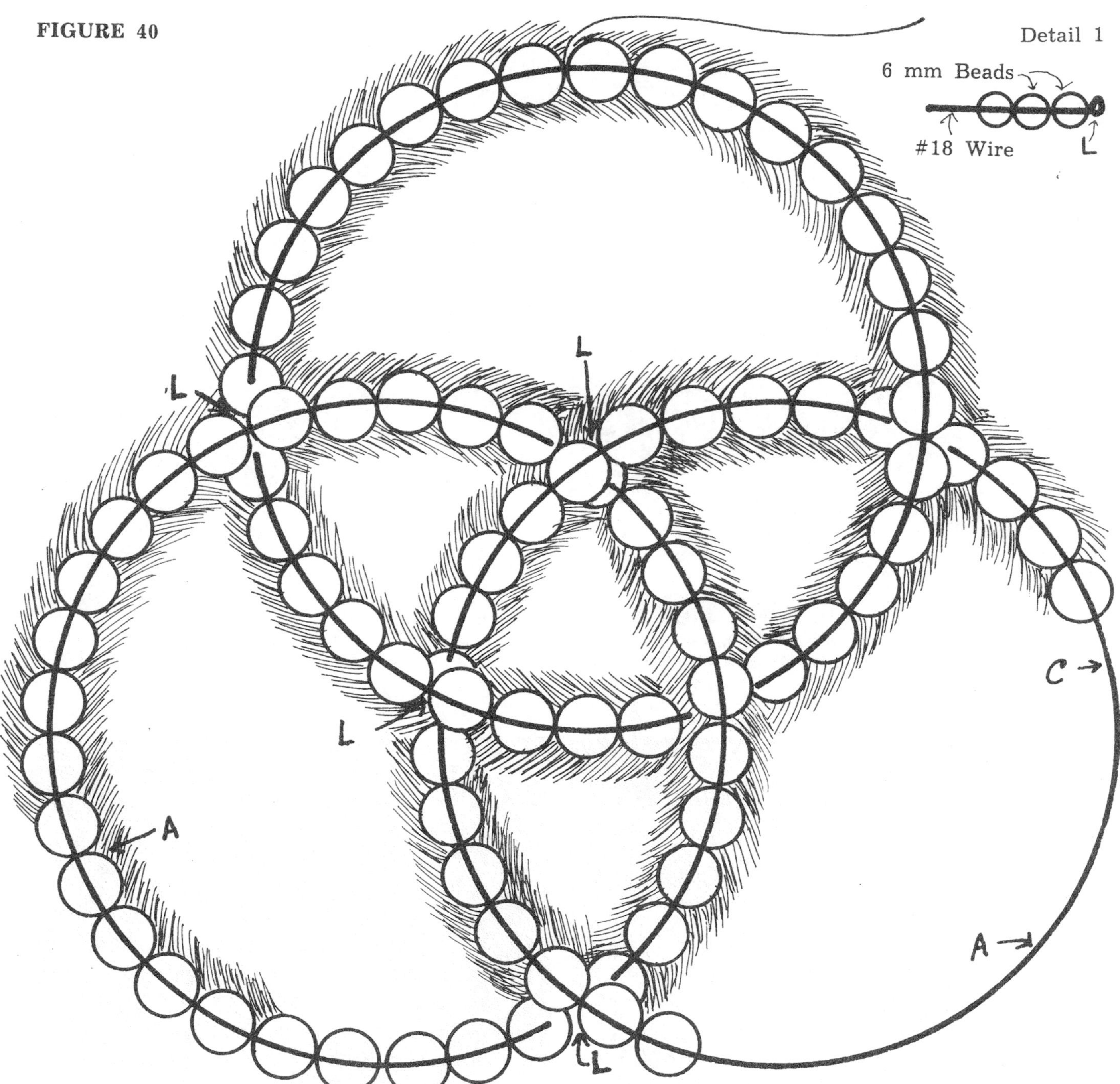

wire, shape three circles to line C. Spiral 1¼ inch gold vinyl festooning onto each circle. (Directions for this procedure are on page 58.) Lay the three rings to fit over the pattern on Figure 40.

Make a tiny loop, L, at the end of a 16 inch piece of #30 gold colored wire. Shape the wire to make a circle the same size as or slightly larger than the stranded wire circle. (Lacing beaded circles through each other shrinks them a little.) String 10 mm gold glass beads to cover the wire circle. Make another loop, L, at the end of the circle to match the first loop. Make two more similar beaded circles.

With #30 wire, fasten the two end L loops together to close two circles. Lay the two closed circles on the pattern so that another beaded ring will cover the L loops; note carefully which ring is atop the other. Weave the still open third circle through the two closed rings to join them as shown on the pattern. Slightly bend the beaded circles so that they flow over each other smoothly. Wire the third ring closed. With pieces of #30 wire, fasten the circles together where they cross over each other. Do NOT cut off the excess wire.

(Continued on page 60.)

CC. FISH BEARING A BASKET OF BREAD

FIGURE 41

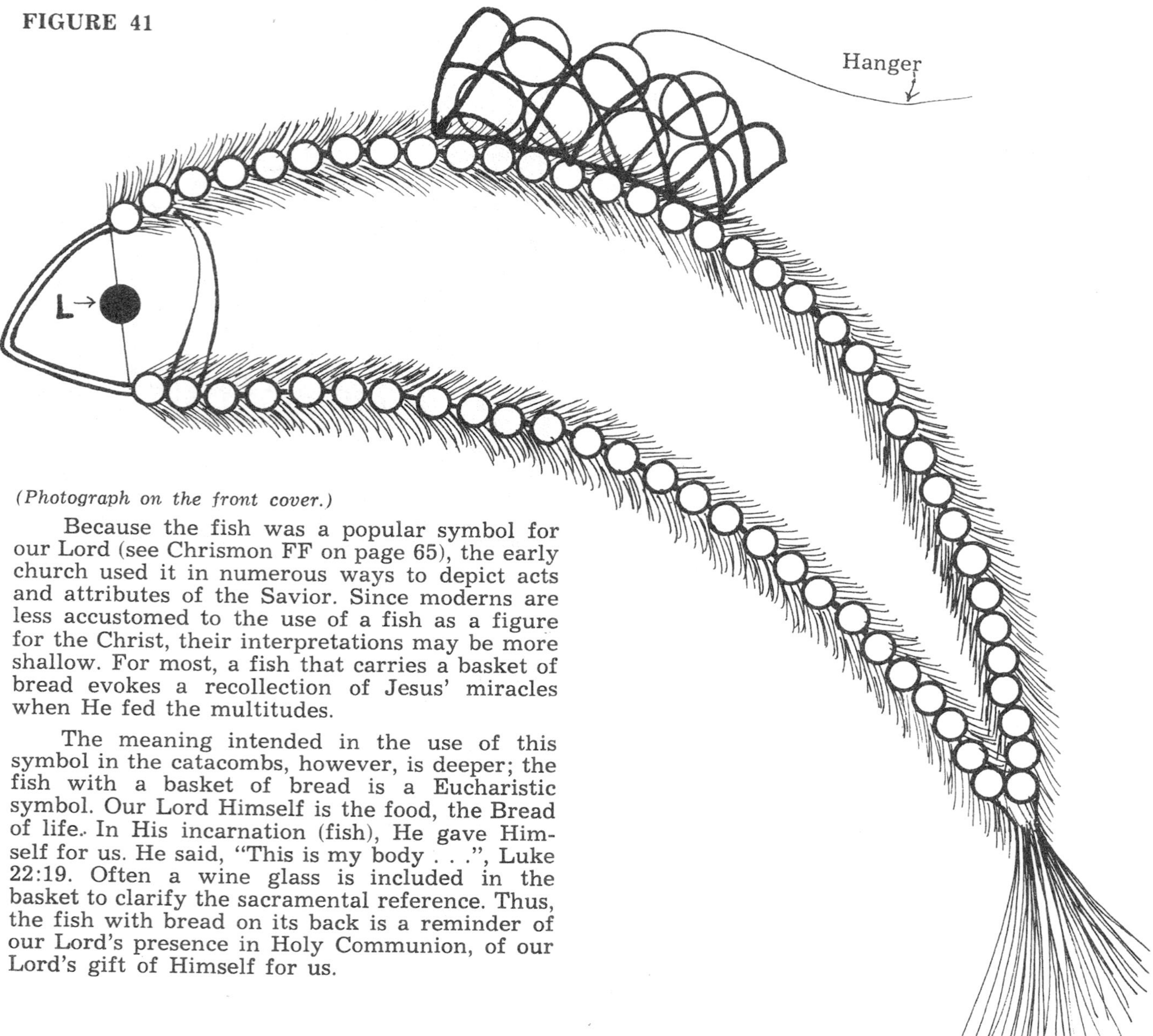

(Photograph on the front cover.)

Because the fish was a popular symbol for our Lord (see Chrismon FF on page 65), the early church used it in numerous ways to depict acts and attributes of the Savior. Since moderns are less accustomed to the use of a fish as a figure for the Christ, their interpretations may be more shallow. For most, a fish that carries a basket of bread evokes a recollection of Jesus' miracles when He fed the multitudes.

The meaning intended in the use of this symbol in the catacombs, however, is deeper; the fish with a basket of bread is a Eucharistic symbol. Our Lord Himself is the food, the Bread of life. In His incarnation (fish), He gave Himself for us. He said, "This is my body . . .", Luke 22:19. Often a wine glass is included in the basket to clarify the sacramental reference. Thus, the fish with bread on its back is a reminder of our Lord's presence in Holy Communion, of our Lord's gift of Himself for us.

DD. THREE FISHES ENTWINED IN A CIRCLE

(Photograph on page 61.)

Since our Savior's activities are easily seen, the tendency is to forget that all three Persons of the Trinity participate in our redemption. One fish symbolizes the second Person of the Triune, the one sacrifice for all of us. Three fishes remind us that three Persons participate in our salvation: The Father loves and gives; the Son is the means; the Spirit calls and enables us to respond.

The triangular aspect of the design emphasizes the fact that, although each Person does His specific work, all Persons act to make a perfect Whole. In the union of these fishes in a circle, we recognize the eternity of the One God.

Note: Figure 42 for Chrismon DD on page 62 diagrams the steps in the construction of the fish which is the basis for Chrismons CC and DD. Except for the basket which is on Chrismon CC only, materials for both Chrismons are the same.

(Continued from page 59.)

Position the beaded rings on the fringed circles; with the #30 wire left over from joining the beaded circles, attach the beaded to the fringed rings. If necessary, make extra attachments on the outside of the figure at points A. Wrap a piece of #30 wire around both circles to make the top hanger. With a needle pull out any pieces of fringe caught by the wires.

Materials: 1″ & 2″ gold vinyl festooning or thick, wide gold tinsel; 6 mm gold glass beads; 8 mm pearls; gold backed paper; 1/8″ diameter stranded wire; #30 hair wire; #18 or #20 gold or copper colored wire; gold paint; white glue.

For Chrismon CC only: Gold plastic doily; white styrofoam.

Directions for Chrismons CC and DD:

From a 21 inch length of stranded wire, shape the outline of the fish to lie between the two pattern lines shown on fish A on Figure 42 on page 62. Lay the wire from H to and through G, D, and E to F; return the wire through the opposite E, D, and G to the opposite H. Cut off the excess wire. Loosen one strand of the wire from each H to G end. Wrap the loosened wires tightly around each other and the other stranded wire to hold the wires to the shape of the fish. Paint the wire fish gold.

Wrap a three inch length of two inch gold vinyl festooning around G to make the tail. Wrap #30 wire tightly around the solid edge of the festooning at G to hold it in so that its fringe flares out to combine with the H wires.

Spiral one inch gold vinyl festooning from G to E on the dorsal (top) side of the fish and from G to E on the ventral (bottom) side. (Directions for this procedure are on page 58.) Trim the fringe to a neat three-fourths inch width.

* * *

Straight line anchor an 8 mm pearl at the middle of a ten inch piece of #30 wire. See Detail 1 on Figure 42 on page 62. Set the wired pearl as the eye between the wires of the head of the fish at the point marked by the large black dot on Figure 42. Wrap and twist the #30 wire ends around the stranded wire at points E. Do NOT cut off the excess #30 wire.

* * *

Bend the end of an 18 inch length of #20 gold or copper colored wire to the shape shown at J on Detail 2 of Figure 42. Loop J will later be pinched around the stranded wire at E. The K extension lifts the #20 wire above the stranded wire to allow room to string the 6 mm beads. Hook loop J over the stranded wire of the fish at an E point. Shape the wire to the fish outline from E through D to G. String 6 mm gold glass beads over the wires to G. Sharply bend the wire at G; shape it through the opposite D to the next E. String the wire with 6 mm glass beads to E. Then bend the wire to loop over the stranded wire at E. With needle nosed pliers pinch loops J around the stranded wire at points E. Twist the #30 wire that was left over from attaching the eye around the #20 wire to hold it at K. Use #30 wire pieces to fasten the beaded wire to the stranded wire at G. If it is needed, fasten the beaded and stranded wires together at points D in the same manner. Cut off the excess #20 and #30 wires.

From two pieces of gold paper glued together with the gold side out or the solid edge of the festooning, cut the gill line by the pattern. Dip the wide end of the gill into white glue. Insert it between the fringe and the beads at M on the pattern. If a smooth finish is wanted, cut one-fourth inch strips of gold backed paper. Spiral and glue the strips around the stranded wire from E, around F, and on to the opposite E to hide the extra wires and fringe ends. With a needle, pull out the ends of any fringe that is caught under the wires.

* * *

To complete Chrismon CC:

Make the basket from a gold plastic doily which is available at notions counters in variety stores. Cut a four inch circle from the doily. Then cut a pie-shaped piece (about one-third of the doily) out of the circle. Loop #30 wire around the pie-cut edges of the remaining two-thirds of the circle to pull those edges together to form a cone. Push the tip of the cone into itself to make the basket more shallow. Wire the bottom closed and, if necessary, wire tucks into the fabric of the basket to complete its shaping.

Attach a #30 wire to the stranded wire on the top D of the fish to make a hanger. Place the basket over the hanger so that it emerges from the center top of the basket. Loop #30 wire around the bottom of the basket and the stranded and/or #20 wire at D to hold the basket in place.

Carve the loaves of bread from white styrofoam. Make each loaf about three-fourths inch in diameter. Pile them into the basket and glue them in place with white glue.

FIGURE 42

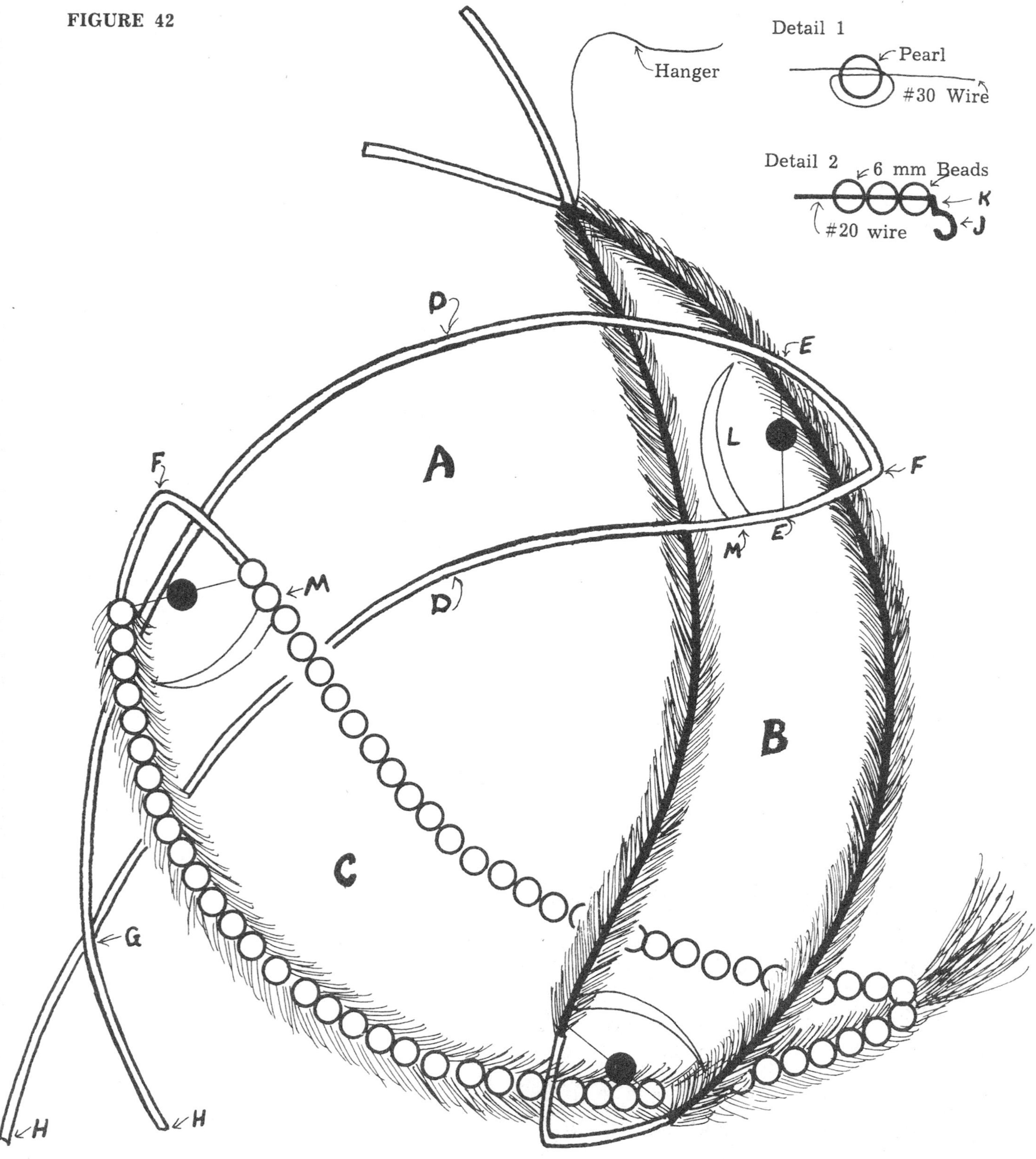

To complete Chrismon DD:

Place three fishes on top of one another as shown on the pattern on Figure 42. Notice that each head is on top of the preceding fish's tail. With #30 wire fasten the fishes together at two or three places where they cross over one another.

Attach #30 wire to a G point to make the hanger as shown. Use a needle to free any fringe that may be caught under the wires.

EE. STYLIZED FISH

(Photograph on this page.)

FIGURE 43

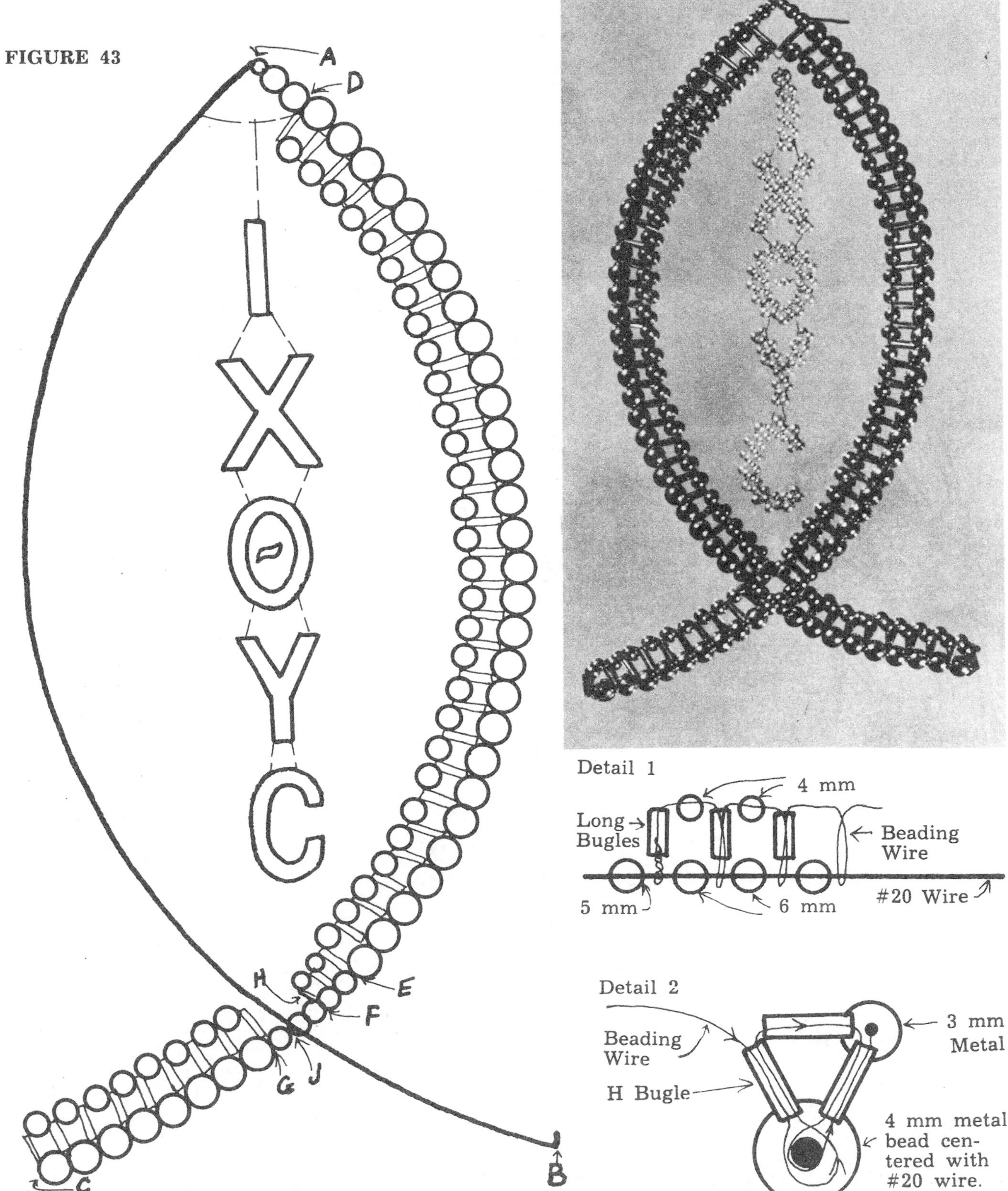

Early Christians used the fish widely as an easily made and recognized secret sign. During the times of the persecution of the church, Christians could find each other by using this simple password. To the outsider, the fish was a mere decoration; to the Christian, it was an affirmation of faith in the Christ.

Centuries after the days of the New Testament church that initiated this symbol, a news story reported that Cuban Christians had revived the use of this emblem. When, in 1963, they found themselves in a situation similar to that faced by the first Christians, the Cubans employthe fish as a secret password just as the early Christians did. (Also see the interpretation for Chrismon FF on page 66.)

Materials: 3, 4, 5, & 6 mm gold metal beads; gold glass bugle beads (if they are available, use extra long bugles); 2 or 2½ mm pearls; #18 or #20 gold or copper colored wire; gold beading wire; #30 hair wire.

Directions:

Shape and bend a 23 inch length of #20 gold or copper colored wire to the outline from B to A to C of the pattern on Figure 43 on page 63. Let the wire extend one inch beyond B and C.

String gold metal beads on the AC wire. Beads from point A down are as follows: One 3 mm, a 4 mm, and a 5 mm bead. This is point D. Then string 6 mm beads until the beads reach point E, which is five-eighths of an inch before the crossover point J. Next string 4 mm beads to point G, one bead past the crossover point J. (The total number of 4 mm beads will generally be five.) Finally, string 6 mm beads to point C. With needle-nosed pliers, twist a little loop in the #20 wire at C to hold the beads on the wire. There should be about 1/8 or 3/16 inch slack on the wire to allow room for crossing the wires at J later. Cut off the excess wire. Bead and end the AB section in the same way.

* * *

Twist the end of a length of gold beading wire around the AC wire at D. See Detail 1 of Figure 43. String a long, gold glass bugle bead, a 4 mm metal bead, and another bugle bead on the beading wire. Loop the beading wire around the AC wire between the first two 6 mm beads. Run the beading wire back through the last bugle bead that was strung. Tighten the beading wire so that the beads are positioned as shown on the pattern and the bugle and 4 mm bead weave stands up straight. The 6 mm beads on the #30 wire will almost touch because they are separated only by the beading wire. The 4 mm beads are separated by the ends of the bugle beads.

Continue to string long bugle and 4 mm beads to point E. At E, gradually shorten the bugles and use 3 mm instead of the 4 mm gold metal beads to point F. After the beading wire has been run back through bead H, string two more bugles on the wire. Again loop the beading wire around the #20 wire at F as shown on Detail 2 of Figue 43. Run the wire back through the bugle opposite H. Tighten the wires.

The wire is now in position to weave another row of bugles and 3 and 4 mm metal beads directly behind the row from D to F. Duplicate the weave from F to D so that it lies behind the beads already woven from D to F. Twist the wire around the beading wire already at D to hold. Do NOT cut off the excess wire. Point the first woven row of beads slightly toward the front, the second row of beads toward the back. This will give depth to the Chrismon.

Bead the AB wire from D to F in the same manner. Then bead the AC wire from G to C with a similar double row of long bugles and 4 mm metal beads. All the bugle beads in this weave are long; all the metal beads are 4 mm in size. Twist beading wire around point J to hold the fish together. Twist a piece of #30 wire around the #20 wire at A to make the hanger.

* * *

Weave the letters to form the *IXΘYC* of 2 or 2½ mm pearls on beading wire. Follow the same pattern that is given for the word on Chrismon FF on pages 65, 66, and 67. Do NOT cut off the leftover beading wires. Instead, use the wires to join the letters to one another as shown by the dashes on the Figure 43 pattern.

Twist the two beading wires that are left over from the weaves at points D together at the center of the fish. Run two wires down to the top of the Iota. Twist the wires around the top weaving wires of the Iota to hold the letters in place at the center of the fish.

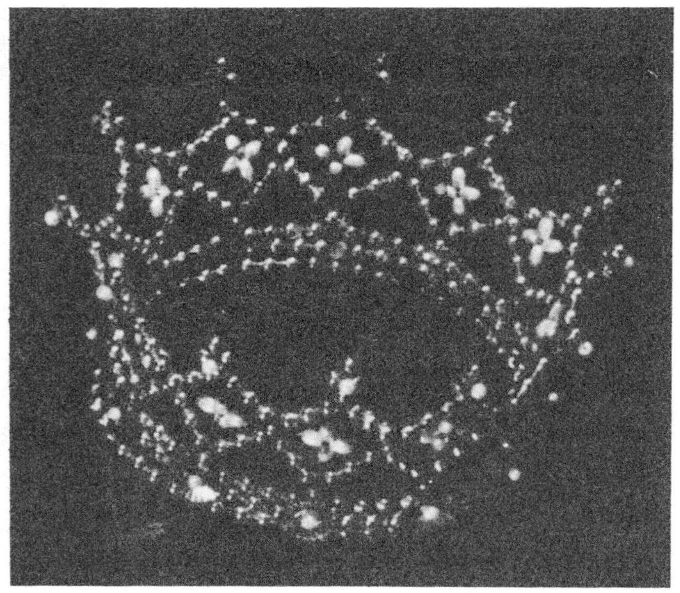

FF. FISH (IXΘYC) IN A CIRCLE

(Photograph on the back cover.)

FIGURE 44

As early as the second century, Christians were using the fish as a symbol for the Christ. Most sources say that the use of this figure developed because the letters of the Greek word for fish, *Ichthus* (*IXΘYC-IXΘYΣ*) formed an acrostic on the Greek phrase, "Jesus Christ, God's Son, Savior." (I—Iota, X—Chi, Θ—Theta, Y—Upsilon, C—Sigma.) A few authorities, however, suggest that, since such a complex of meanings centered around the fish (His miracles, His fishermen disciples, the curiosity of a being who could live in an element—water—in which man dies, among other ideas of that age and culture), it was a symbol first; the acrostic was worked out later.

Clement of Alexandria recommended the design of a fish as suitable for Christians to use on jewelry. In the catacombs, fishes were drawn on the walls to direct worshipers to meeting places. Devotional and inspirational carvings made frequent use of fishes in several ways. A fish not only symbolized the Christ in various acts but it also referred to His teachings, explained doctrine and even, when a number of small fishes were used, represented the followers of the Christ, the Christian community. Use of the fish was and is a strong confession of faith and an affirmation of the basic doctrine of Christianity. Also see the interpretations for Chrismons CC, DD, and EE.

Materials: ½" white styrofoam; styrofoam glue; 5 mm gold sequins-by-the-yard; gold sequin material or gold-backed paper; 10 & 16 mm gold glass beads; 3 & 6 mm pearls; gold paint; gold sequin pins; #18 & #14 stiff florist wire; #20 gold or copper colored wire; #30 hair wire; gold beading wire.

Directions:

Cut out two fishes from one-half inch thick white styrofoam by the pattern of the fish's head and body on Figure 44 on page 65. Do not include the fins in the cutout. Place the two fishes together; match the heads and the tails. Fasten the two fishes together temporarily by running two pipe cleaner pieces through the body behind the head. Carve and shape the styrofoam to a rounded body and head of a fish. Some of the modeling may be done by pressing the foam to the desired shape with the fingers. Indent the mouth by pressing the foam in with the dull side of a paring knife. Press a 6 mm pearl into the foam on each side of the head as a setting for the eyes. Separate the fish into its two halves.

From gold sequin material or two pieces of gold-backed paper glued together with the gold sides out, cut out the fins shown on the pattern on Figure 44. Each fin pattern includes the visible striped section bordered with a solid line and the dashed line section that is hidden in the styrofoam. Cut out one each of the dorsal, ventral, and tail fins. Cut out two gill fins. With a stylus or ball point pen, score the fins along the parallel stripes.

Spread styrofoam glue over the inside of the two halves of the body of the fish. Place the fins, except the gill fins, between the two halves of the body. If necessary, hold the fins in place by running sequin pins through the fin into the body. Wrap cord around the body of the fish to hold the two parts and the fins in place until the glue is dry.

Cover the fins of the fish with masking tape. Spray the entire fish with gold styrofoam paint. (Follow the paint directions carefully. Ordinary paint melts styrofoam.) When the paint is dry, remove the masking tape. Cover the entire body of the fish from headline to tail fin with 5 mm gold sequins-by-the-yard. Glue and pin one row of sequins to the body at a time. Run a row from the head to the tail along the center top and the bottom lines of the body. Add extra rows of sequins in the wider midsection of the fish and taper off the rows at the narrower tail section. After the body is covered with sequins, cut a slice in each side with a little pointed knife to accept the gill fins. Cover the end of each fin with white glue; insert it into the body in the position shown on the pattern.

While the gold paint finish is a satisfactory background for the sequins, the head may be too rough in appearance. Paint the head (all the fish not covered by sequins) with a heavy coat of styrofoam glue. After the glue is completely dry, sand the rough places smooth. Paint the head with another coat of glue. Sand the head again. Apply a third coat of glue. (Individual preference determines the number of coats of glue and sandings that are done. Extra coats of glue lead to a smoother finish; fewer coats of glue results in a rougher—although in some cases a satisfactory—surface. The glue coating also serves to protect the styrofoam so that it will take ordinary paint without melting. Use this process whenever smooth styrofoam or a painted surface is desired. Always end with a coat of glue.) When the last coat of glue is thoroughly dry, paint the head with a good quality metallic gold paint. Gold metallic leaf may be applied over the paint. Follow the directions that come with the leaf.

Cut two curved strips of gold sequin material or gold-backed paper to fit on each side of the fish between the head and the body. Pin and glue the strips in place as shown on the pattern. Glue a 6 mm pearl in place for each eye. Run a needle threaded with green or black thread through the upper part of the dorsal fin at K. Tie a knot at one end of the thread so that it does not pull through the hole in the fin.

* * *

Shape A, the wire support for the letters, from #18 stiff green florist wire. Follow the pattern on Figure 44 for this A support.

Weave the letters of *IXΘYC* of 3 mm pearls on beading wire. Figure 45 on page 67 diagrams the weave and the number of beads in each letter. Curves in the Theta and Sigma are woven into the letters by using slightly smaller beads on the

FIGURE 45

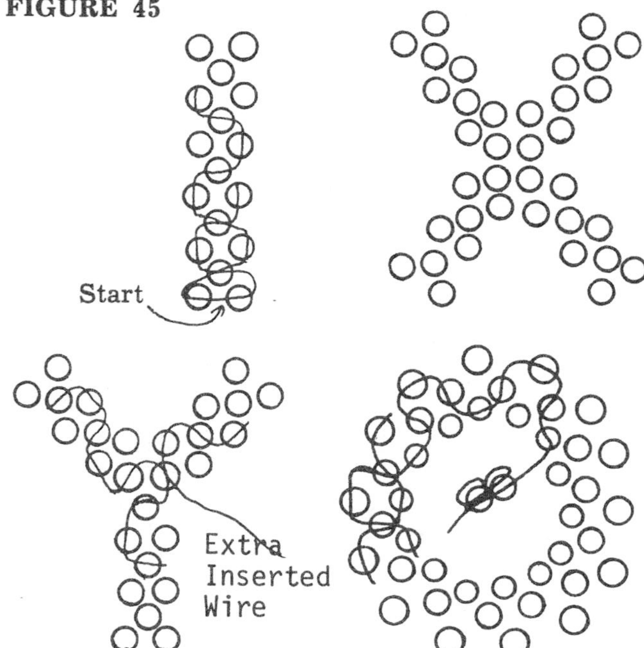

inner line of the curve and slightly larger beads on the outer line. Before the letters are woven, sort the 3 mm pearls to select about 30 extra large and the same number of smaller than average beads. Reserve these beads to use in the construction of the Theta and Sigma.

Do not cut off the wires left over from weaving the letters. Instead, either leave them at the end of the weave at the top and/or bottom of the letters, or backweave the wires so that they are at the top and/or bottom. Fasten the letters to support wire A by twisting the leftover beading wires around wire A. Then cut off the excess weaving wires. When additional attachment wires are needed, run extra pieces of beading wire through the end beads of the letters to twist around wire A.

* * *

The frame for the outer circle of beads is #14 stiff green florist wire which is shaped to an 8 1/8 inch diameter circle. Bend a little loop at the end of a piece of #14 wire as shown at L on Figure 46 on this page. Then shape the wire to circle D on the Figure 44 pattern on page 65. The end of the wire should lap over the beginning of the circle for at least an inch. The wire must fit the circle exactly before any beads are strung; trying to shape the wire after beads are on it will result in crushing them.

The circular frame is composed of two rows of beads: The outer row of 16 mm gold glass beads is strung on the #14 wire. The inner row of 10 mm gold glass beads is on #30 wire which also runs through the outer 16 mm beads. Both beaded circles are woven at one time. Follow Figures 46 and 44 to make these circles.

To begin the weave, twist the end of a five foot length of #30 wire to hold around loop L. Run a 16 mm bead, M, over both the #14 and the #30 wires. Push the bead tight against loop L. String a 10 mm bead, G on Figure 46 on this page, on the #30 wire only. String another 16 mm bead, F, over both wires; push it against the previously strung 16 mm bead. Position the 10 mm bead G close to the junction of the 16 mm beads with the hole of the 10 mm bead parallel to the #14 wire D. Pull out and tighten the #30 wire. Hold the #30 and #14 wires with one hand; with the other hand, turn bead G so that the #30 wire that goes into and out of G twists on itself to anchor bead G in place. String another 10 mm bead, E, on the #30 wire only; run another 16 mm F bead over both wires. Push the beads tight and turn bead E to anchor it. Continue to string 10 and 16 mm beads around the circle in the same manner. The 16 mm beads should touch one another around the circle.

When the circle is beaded to point C on Figure 44, gently work the C end of support wire A through the holes of the 16 mm beads on circle D. Twist the #30 wire around the #14 and #18 wires at C to hold the circle and support wires together. Continue to bead the circle with 16 and 10 mm beads. At B, again twist the #30 wire around wires A and D to hold them together. When the beading of D continues, run the 16 mm beads over wires D, A, and the #30 wire.

After bead N, the last 16 mm bead, is strung and before P, the last 10 mm bead is placed, bend a loop at the end of the #14 wire to match loop L. Two strong pliers, one on the #14 wire between the beads and the end loop and the other to bend the wire, can do the job without crushing the beads. String and anchor bead P. Twist the #30 wire around the two loops to close circle D. The leftover #30 wire is the hanger.

Shape a 26 inch length of #20 gold or copper colored wire to circle H (about 7 3/8 inches in diameter) on Figure 44. The ends of the circle lap over each other. Gently insert the wire through the holes of the 10 mm beads around the circle. Lap the #20 wire in the end beads.

* * *

Run a piece of beading wire through each of the two 10 mm beads, Q, that are in front of support wire A. Twist each end of the beading wire around A to hold the support wire tightly against beads Q. Run the thread from the fish at K through bead P. Tie the thread at J to hold the fish in its position on Figure 44. The thread enables the fish to move independently of the circle when the Chrismon is hung.

FIGURE 46

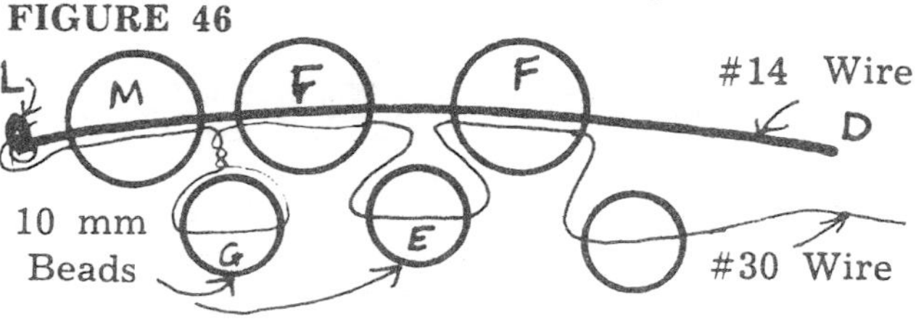

X P
CHI RHO

FIGURE 47

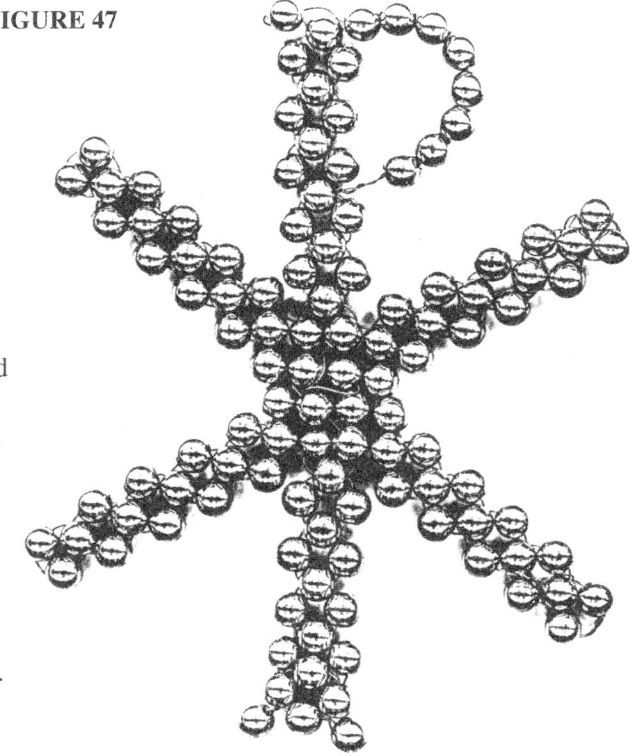

113 OF 5mm Beads

Make the CHI first.
Cut about 14 inches of #28 gold beading wire. Center first bead on wire. Add bead to L &R Wire. Make a crossover in the R bead. This forms a square edge for the CHI. Add L&R bead. Add a bead to R wire. Run L wire through bead forming a CROSS-OVER. Make 12 CROSSOVERS (count center bead). End with a bead on L&R wire. CROSSOVER in the R bead. Back weave to finish with a square end,

Start the next arm the same way. Make 5 CROSSOVERS. End with a bead on L&R wire. Thread the L wire through CROSS-OVER bead #6, R wire through bead #7 of the first arm. Add a bead to the L&R wires. Make 5 CROSSOVERS. Square off end. CHI is completed.

Make RHO
Cut 18 inches of wire. To make wide footing of the RHO see page 31 of Basic Series. Make 6 CROSSOVERS. This is tricky... weave L&R wire through center of X. Continue for 6 CROSS-OVERS. Add L&R bead.

To form the P, Run the L wire through the R bead. String 6 beads on the double wire. Put I bead on single wire. Bring the two wires together and twist wire for about 1/4 inch. Run 1 wire through #4 CROSSOVER from the top of the P. Twist the two wires in back. Add hanger (8 in. Wire through top CROSSOVER bead, twist. Wrap long wire around pencil.)

SEE PAGE 20 OF BASIC SERIES

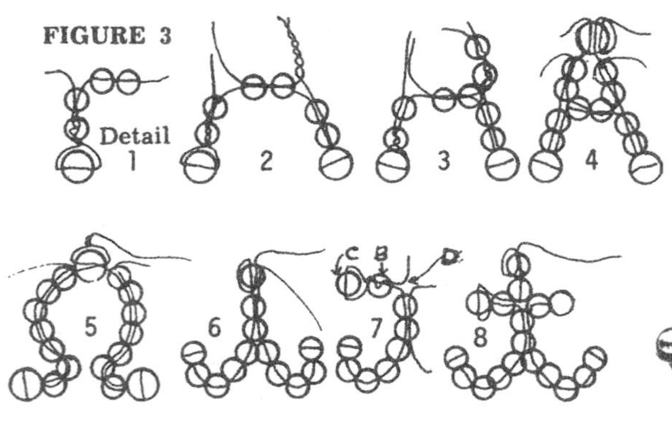

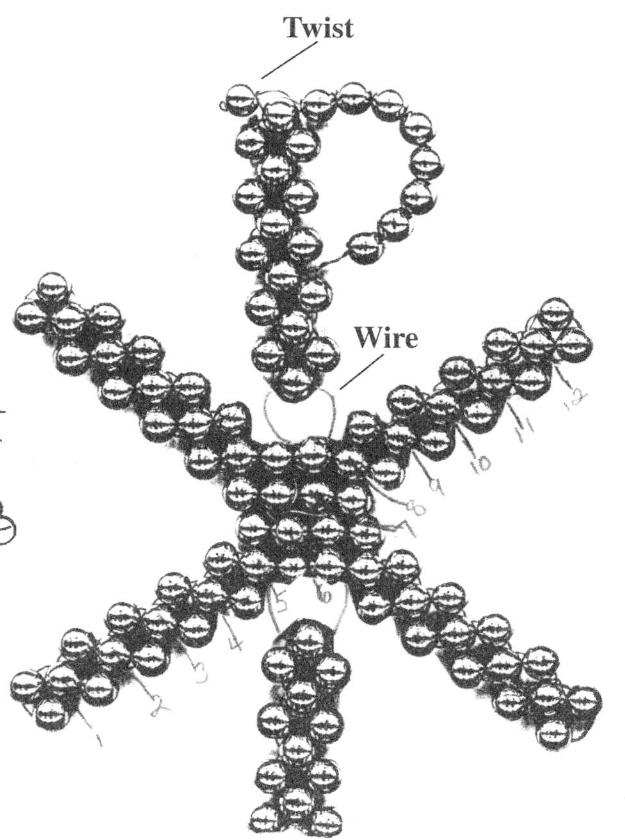

SUBMITTED BY: MARTHA GRAY MCCAULEY

Holy Spirit Descending Dove

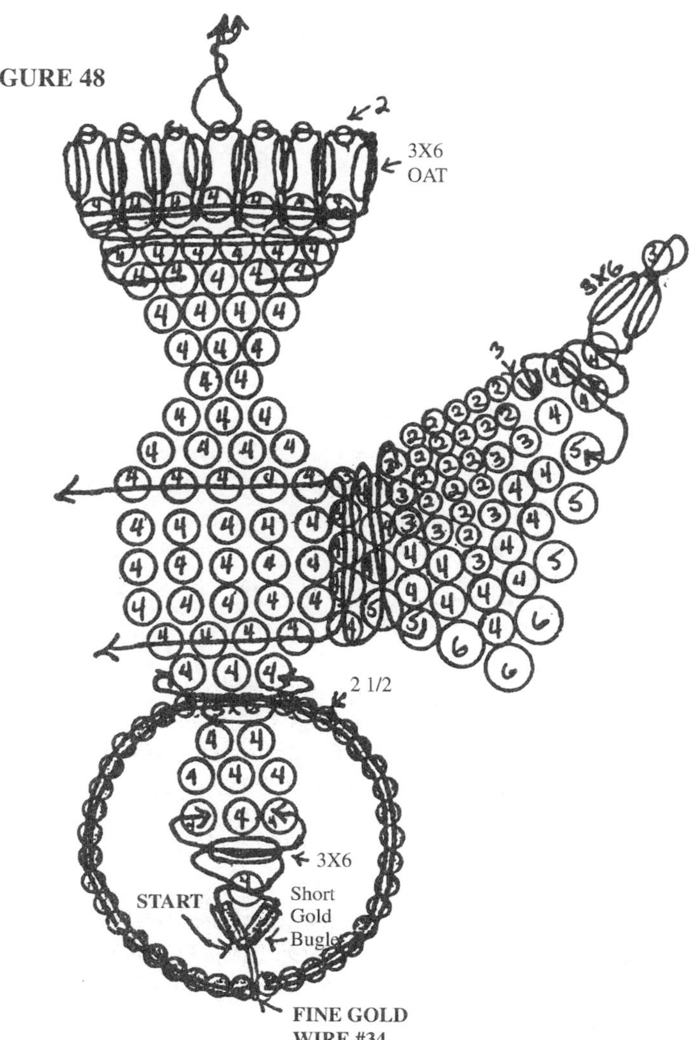

MATERIALS NEEDED:

#30 WIRE	2 PIECES 44"
	1 PIECE 12"
#34 GOLD WIRE	
	1 PIECE 4"
BEADS	2 SHORT GOLD BUGLES
	36 2 1/2mm GOLD
	14 3X6mm PEARL
	43 2mm PEARL
	24 3mm PEARL
	112 4mm PEARL
	10 5mm PEARL
	6 6mm PEARL

BODY: String 2 gold bugles on a 44" wire long. Thread both ends of the wire through opposite ends of a 4mm pearl bead crossing wire inside bead. Center beads on wire. Cross wires in 3x6mm pearl bead just as wires were crossed in the 4mm bead. Continue crossing wires row by row as shown in the diagram until the last row of 7 4mm pearl beads has been completed. Add 3x6mm oat pearls to each wire; then add a 2mm pearl and another 3x6mm oat pearl to each wire. Wrap wires around the wires between the first and second 4mm pearl on each end on the last row of 7 - 4mm pearl beads. Thread wire back up through the last 3x6mm oat pearl on wires and pull tight. Continue in this manner, adding a 2 mm pearl, 3x6mm oat pearl, wrapping around the wire and rethreading the oat pearl until center is reached. Cross wires through the last 2mm pearl and twist for a hanger.

WINGS: Beginning at the wing tip, string 1 - 3mm pearl on a 44" wire; center and twist wire enough to hold a bead in place. Add 1 - 3x6mm oat pearl to each wire and cross wires through a 4mm pearl bead. Continue crossing wires through each progressive row carefully noting the size of the beads shown in the diagram. One must shape the wing as rows are added. When the last row of 3 - 4mm pearl and 2 - 3mm pearl beads has been completed, thread wires through body of dove as illustrated. Work the second wing from the body to the tip in the reverse order as the first wing. Finish wing by working wires back into the beads already strung.

HALO: String 36 - 21/2mm gold beads on a wire 12" long. Cross the wires through the 3X6mm oat pearl in neck of dove. Go back through all the gold beads and the oat pearl; end by working wire into beads of the body. Connect beak and halo with 4" piece of #34 gold wire

SUBMITTED BY: FRIENDS OF CHRISMONS

Anchor Cross (Cross of Hope)

CHRISTMAS: This Child, the hope of the world. Or, a cross rises out of the crescent moon, a symbol for Mary, our Lord's mother.

Materials:

18 - 2mm pearl	36 - 3mm pearl	6 - 4mm pearl	20 - 5mm pearl
2 - 6mm pearl	1 - 8mm pearl	2 - 18" wire, 28 ga.	1 - 12" wire, 28 ga.

FIGURE 49

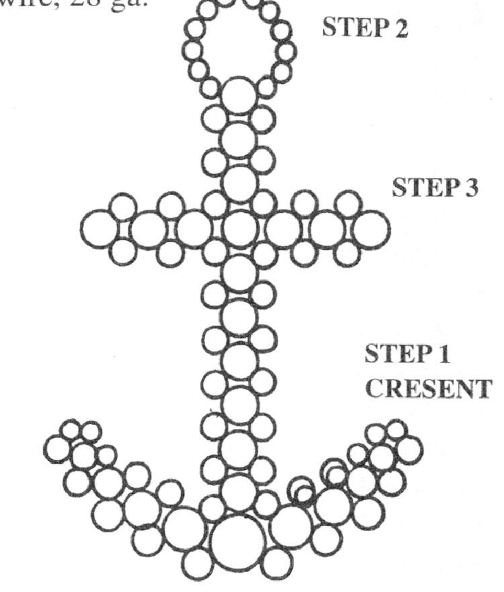

Step 1 Center a 2mm pearl on an 18" wire. Put a 2mm pearl on one wire and a 3mm pearl on the other. Cross-connect (CC) a 3mm pearl. (From this point, remember which are the inner and outer sides of the crescent!) Put a 2mm pearl on the inner wire (the same side as the first 2mm pearl), a 3mm pearl on the outer wire and CC a 4mm pearl. Put a 3mm pearl on the inner wire, a 4mm pearl on the outer wire and CC a 5mm pearl. Put a 3mm pearl on the inner wire, a 5mm pearl on the outer wire, and CC a 6mm pearl.

Put a 4mm pearl on the inner wire, a 5mm pearl on the outer wire and CC an 8mm pearl. Put a 4mm pearl on the inner wire, a 5mm pearl on the outer wire, and CC a 6mm pearl. Put a 3mm pearl on the inner wire, a 5mm pearl on the outer wire and CC a 5mm pearl. Put a 3mm, pearl on the inner wire, a 4mm pearl on the outer wire, and CC a 4mm pearl. Put a 2mm pearl on the inner wire, a 3mm pearl on the outer wire and CC a 3mm pearl. Put a 2mm pearl on the inner wire, a 3mm pearl on the outer wire, and CC a 2mm pearl. Secure and trim wires. This completes the crescent, lay aside.

BEGIN CROSS

Step 2 Form a hanger eye in an 18" wire. Put six (6) 2mm pearls on each side of the hanger eye, CC a 5mm pearl. Put a 3mm pearl on each wire and CC a 5mm pearl. Repeal eight (8) more CC's. DO NOT SECURE OR TRIM WIRES. This completes the upright. The wires will be used to attach the cross to the anchor.

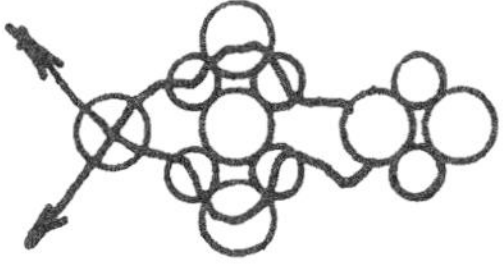

ATTACH CROSS ARM

Step 3 Center a 5mm pearl on the 12" wire. Put a 3mm pearl on each wire and CC a 5mm pearl. Repeat one (1) more CC. Attach the cross arm to the upright at the fourth 5 mm pearl from the top. On the other side of the upright, CC a 5mm pearl. Put a 3mm pearl on each wire and CC a 5mm pearl. Repeat one (1) more CC. Secure and trim wires.

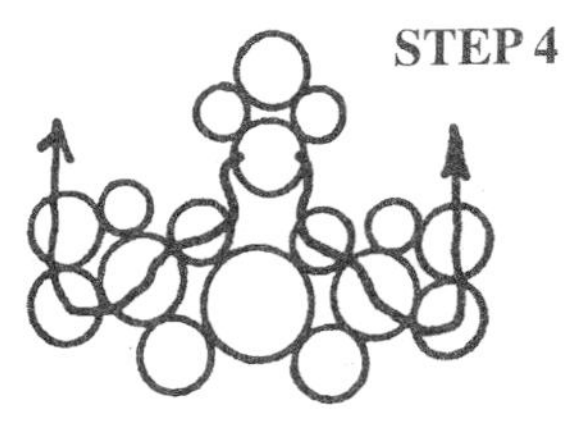

ATTACH CROSS TO CRESENT

Step 4 Attach the cross to the inside of the crescent at the 8mm pearl. Thread the wires outward through the 4mm pearls, downward through the 6mm pearls, outward through the 5mm pearls, and upward through the 5mm pearls, trim wires.

SUBMITTED BY: FRANK GRAHAM PRITCHARD

Cross of Constantine

4 - 6mm pearl	8 - 3x6mm gold
3 - 4mm pearl	1 - 18" wire, 28 ga.
31 - 3mm pearl	1 - 15" wire, 28 ga.
64 - 3mm gold	1 - 12" wire, 28 ga.

FIGURE 50

The Chi Rho with the X turned to form a cross - Christ the victorious King

Upright:
- Form a hanger eye in the 18" wire
- Cross-connect (CC) a 3mm pearl
- Put a 3mm gold on one wire and a 3mm pearl on the other wire and CC a 3mm pearl
- Put a 3mm gold on each wire and CC a 3mm pearl
- Repeat above step one (1) more time
- Put a 3mm gold on the same side as the 1st 3mm gold and a 3mm pearl on the same side as the 1st 3mm pearl and CC a 3mm pearl
- Put a 3mm gold on each wire and CC a 3mm pearl
- Put a 3mm gold on each wire and CC a 6mm pearl
- Put a 3mm gold on each wire and CC a 3mm pearl
- Repeat the above step (9) more times
- Put a 3mm gold on each wire and CC a 4mm pearl
- Put a 3mm gold an each wire and CC a 6mm pearl
- Put a 3mm gold on each wire and thread the wires back thru the 6mm pearl
- Trim wires

HANGER EYE

STARTING UPRIGHT

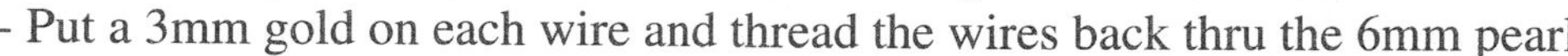

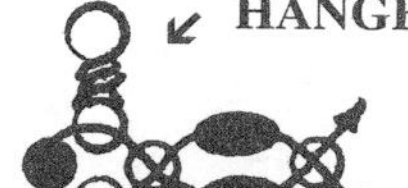

STARTING BOW OF RHO

Bow of RHO:
- Thread the 12" wire per diagram to start bow
- Put a 3x6mm gold on each wire and CC a 3mm pearl
- Put a 3x6mm gold on the outside wire, a 3mm gold on the inside wire and CC a 3mm pearl
- Repeat the above step three (3) more times
- Put a 3x6mm gold on each wire and CC thru the 2nd 3mm pearl on the side
- Thread the wires thru the upright per ending diagram and trim wires

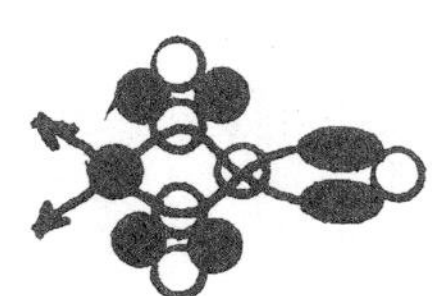

ENDING BOW OF RHO

Crossarm:
- Center a 6mm pearl on the 15" wire
- Put a 3mm gold on each wire and thread each wire back thru 6mm pearl
- Put a 3mm gold on each wire and CC a 4mm pearl
- Put a 3mm gold on each wire and CC a 3mm pearl
- Repeat above step three (3) more times
- Attach the crossarm at the 6mm pearl below the RHO bow
- CC a 3mm pearl on the other side of the upright
- Put a 3mm gold on each wire and CC a 3mm pearl
- Repeat the above step two (2) more times
- Put a 3mm gold on each wire and CC a 4mm pearl
- Put a 3mm gold on each wire and CC a 6mm pearl
- Put a 3mm gold on each wire and thread back thru 6mm pearl and trim wires

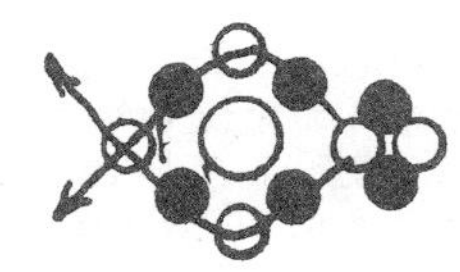

ATTACHING CROSSARM

SUBMITTED BY: FRANK GRAHAM PRITCHARD

OTHER CHRISMON BOOKS AVAILABLE

CHRISMONS FOR EVERY DAY

This most recent of the Chrismon books was released in the autumn of 1971. It is recommended for beginners, intermediate, and advanced Chrismon workers. Beginners will find it a valuable supplement to the *Basic Series* because *Chrismons for Every Day* offers new construction methods for learners and complete and specific workshop guides and outlines. Intermediate and advanced workers as well as beginners will find detailed directions and patterns for miniatures in this book. In addition, any Chrismon maker will be interested in the more than thirty new patterns for medium and large tree decorations. There are crosses, monograms, and symbols—all combined in different ways—as well as a set of eight Chrismons, the Beatitudes. Ornaments vary from very easy to difficult to make.

The main focus of *Chrismons for Every Day,* however, is on demonstrating inspirational uses for these Christian symbols throughout the year. Among the pictured suggestions for which patterns and directions are given are hangings, arrangements, mobiles, pictures, shadowboxes, wedding cake toppers, wreaths, and bookmarks.

As with all the Chrismon books, complete interpretations for all the designs in this book are given. Since these Chrismons were developed a few years after the last previous book, new materials and finishes which hobbyists will enjoy using make up some of the new designs. A number of the pictures of the finished Chrismons are in color.

CHRISMONS: CHRISTIAN YEAR SERIES

The large double loop, or figure 8, that has appeared on the front of the original Chrismon tree since 1960 is the Christian Year Series. This group of Chrismons explains our Lord's life and the nature of the Godhead within the framework of the Liturgical Year. It can be used, as it is at Ascension Church, as a unit to provide a focal point for the tree; or, the individual Chrismons and crosses that compose the Series can hang on a tree in the same manner as the designs in the *Basic Series.*

The emphasis in this group of Chrismons is on symbols and crosses; in fact, no monograms appear. The lamb and the pelican, the gladiolus and the vine, as well as many other ancient and cherished symbols for God—our Lord, the Father, and the Spirit—are used. While each of the designs in the group has its own historical interpretation, its use with the others in the set gives it new and deeper meanings.

By using the Chrismons of the Christian Year as a theme, one can tell a connected story about our Lord and God not only at Christmas time but throughout the year. It has been used as a teaching aid on many occasions for groups both in and outside the church. The instructions include a complete interpretation, which has been used as the basis for Christmas worship programs. In addition to the church size patterns, reduced size patterns for home use are included for all the designs.

Instructions for the Christian Year Series were revised and reprinted in 1972. The new edition includes color photographs of the Series.

CHRISMONS: ADVANCED SERIES

This Series is composed of both individual Chrismons (as in the Basic book) and groups or sets of Chrismons. While the individual ornaments in these sets are related to each other in meaning and are somewhat similar in design, they are not physically connected as are the Chrismons of the Christian Year Series. The whole set need not be constructed or used. Two of the several groups included are the "Angels and Archangels" and the "Parable Balls." Some of the single Chrismons are the "Crown of Thorns," "Wheat and Grapes," "Palms," and various crosses not in either of the other Series.

Only one size pattern is given in this Series. Over half the Chrismons in it, however, are suitable for either home or church use. The designs range from easy to very difficult to make. The worship program in the *Advanced Series* makes use of Chrismons from the *Basic, Christian Year,* and *Advanced Series.* By only a slight change, the *Christian Year Series* group can be omitted.

The instructions for the *Advanced Series* were revised and reprinted during the spring of 1973. The printing includes photographs, some in color, of all the Chrismons in the Series.

No Chrismon designs or patterns are duplicated in any of the Series. The cost of each of the above books as well as of this book, *Chrismons: Basic Series,* can be found on the enclosed information sheet. This price includes the postage.

CHRISMONS FOR CHILDREN

Many of you have asked over the years about something for the children relating to the Chrismons Tree. We are happy to announce the publishing of a children's storybook, in color, ***Samuel Sparrow and The Tree of Light.*** This is wonderful story and a must for all children. This is a perfect gift for that special child in your life. (23pgs.) 8 1/2 x 6 1/2 ISBN # 0-9715472-5-4 - Library of Congress # 2003107199

CHRISMONS

The book which is simply titled *Chrismons* contains condensed interpretations of all the ornaments on the tree at The Lutheran Church of the Ascension in Danville, Virginia. A full color photograph of the tree is on the cover while drawings and photographs of some of the Chrismons illustrate the explanations. This book is arranged in such a way that it is also a handy reference on Christian symbolism.

ISBN 0-9715472-0-3
90000
9780971547209